To Toby,

The Best!

Dick Brett

BOSTON
Inspirational Women

Photographs by Bill Brett and Kerry Brett

Text by Carol Beggy
Foreword by Karen Kaplan

three
bean press

Boston, Inspirational Women
Published by:
Three Bean Press, LLC
P.O. Box 301711
Jamaica Plain, MA 02130
info@threebeanpress.com • www.threebeanpress.com

Publishers Cataloging-in-Publication Data
Brett, Bill
Brett, Kerry
Boston, Inspirational Women / by Bill Brett and Kerry Brett. Carol Beggy.
p. cm.
Summary: Father-and-daughter photographers Bill Brett and Kerry Brett showcase
portraits of more than 120 of Boston's most remarkable women.

ISBN 978-0-9767276-7-5
[1. Photography of women—Nonfiction. 2. Boston women—Nonfiction.
3. Boston—Nonfiction. 4. Women—Nonfiction. 5. Bill Brett—Nonfiction.
6. Kerry Brett—Nonfiction. 7. Photography—Nonfiction. 8. Portraits—Nonfiction.]
I. Beggy, Carol. II. Title.
LCCN 2011931463

Typeset in Verdana

Printed and bound in Guangzhou, China, by Everbest Printing Company, Ltd.,
through Four Colour Print Group in August 2011. Batch 101146

10 9 8 7 6 5 4 3 2 1

Front cover: model Arianna Brown appears courtesy of Maggie Inc.;
hair: Danielle Mignosa; makeup: Dianna Quagenti; stylist: Sarah Hill Richmond;
designer: Michael De Paulo; accessories: Elisha Daniels and Seams Couture;
shoot coordinated by: Nicole Aiguier; portrait by Kerry Brett.
Back cover: Shannon Cook; portrait by Bill Brett.

Cover and book design by Julie Decedue Kelly, Three Bean Press

Dedicated to Carol Beggy

We have been fortunate to collaborate with writer Carol Beggy on this book, as well as three other books about leading Bostonians. A skilled reporter, deft editor, and master organizer of details both large and small, Carol's words tell the stories of the hundreds of people photographed since the first book project began back in 2005. Carol's thorough reporting and concise style reflect the skills of a veteran journalist who has spent her career in New England newsrooms, including a decade at *The Boston Globe*. About four months after we began this book, Carol was diagnosed with thymoma, a rare disease that strikes an estimated 300 people annually. Carol has courageously endured diagnosis, surgery, recuperation, and rigorous physical and occupational therapy in order to regain the use of her extremities, specifically her hands. Carol the writer has shown us Carol the fighter; she is quite simply one of the toughest people you could ever meet. Her tenacity has helped her fight the disease and enabled us to finish this book as we started it—together. Through it all, Carol has applied the same dedication to battling her illness as she has to checking the facts behind every story in every book. While working on this volume focused on Boston's inspirational women, Carol has enriched us with her friendship and *inspired* us with her bravery. It is only fitting that we dedicate this book to her.

—Bill Brett and Kerry Brett

Foreword

When Bill Brett first asked me to write the foreword for *Boston, Inspirational Women*, I naturally thought that this would be a fine and inspiring work for my daughter to see, giving her countless examples of women who are not only extraordinarily successful but who have also made the important choice to help others in life.

But as I thought about it more, something else came to mind:

What about my son?

Wouldn't he benefit from reading the following pages and getting a glimpse into the lives of exceptional people who act for the greater good? Should a simple matter of X and Y chromosomes preclude him from appreciating these individuals who inspire all of us?

The answer, of course, is no. Because while Bill Brett and his daughter Kerry Brett have brought us a beautiful and unique book about the women of Boston, they have also brought us much more. This is a book about the importance of community and how selfless contributions impact the way we work and live every day. It's a wonderful narrative of social consciousness, demonstrating how people put the needs of others above their own personal ambitions. And yes, these people happen to be women. But this is not a women's story. It's a story about all of us. As John F. Kennedy said, "we all inhabit this small planet. We all breathe the same air." And our own little piece of the planet, right here in Boston, is where we can collectively look after each other, inspire each other, and help each other live a life that has virtue and importance.

Of course, nobody brings us the story of Boston better than Bill Brett, who is not just a photographer; he's a documentarian. He understands, intuitively, that the camera doesn't just capture an image, but an entire story. In this book, he is joined by one of the most special women in his life, his daughter Kerry. Together, they bring us nearly 125 revealing portraits of women from all walks of life. And what you hold in your hands is just the beginning.

As Bill said to me, "I'd need 10 more books to showcase all the inspirational women in Boston. I'm glad my daughter is young, because she can continue this new series." In a city filled with tradition, that's one legacy we'd like to see continued. And I am honored to welcome you to the beginning of this wonderful journey.

This book is truly special. But I think one of the most illuminating aspects of this entire project happened before it was even done. As Bill and Kerry were taking these photographs, each of the women would say, "Hey, you know who else you should put in this book?" There you have it. No turf wars, no overriding self-interest. Just a natural and inherent sense of community, thinking about others and understanding how we are all interconnected. For me, this is a perfect example of what the women in this book are really all about. They realize that what truly matters in life is the contribution, not the recognition, and I have found them to be a source of genuine inspiration. But don't take my word for it.

Ask my son.

—*Karen Kaplan*

Biographies

Bill Brett has been an award-winning photojournalist for close to half a century, spending much of that time at *The Boston Globe*, which he joined as a part-time photographer at age 18. *The Globe* twice named him its director of photography, in 1977 and again in 1999. After taking a company-offered buyout in 2001, Bill has continued to contribute to the newspaper's pages while producing four books—*Boston, All One Family*; *Boston, An Extended Family*; *Boston, A Year in the Life*; and now *Boston, Inspirational Women*. The first three proved to be best sellers for Commonwealth Editions. This is his first publication with Three Bean Press. Bill and Carol Beggy shared the 2006 President's Award from the Urban League of Eastern Massachusetts for their work on *Boston, All One Family*. And in 2009 Bill received an honorary degree from the Benjamin Franklin Institute of Technology, where he took his only class in photography more than 40 years ago. Bill lives in Hingham, Massachusetts, with his wife, Virginia. They have four children and three grandchildren with a fourth on the way.

In her first collaboration with her father, **Kerry Brett**, the staff photographer for *The Improper Bostonian* for 17 years and counting, brings a singular editorial style that is reflected prominently in the celebrity portraits that appear on the covers of this twice-monthly magazine. A renowned portrait photographer, she is the owner of Kerry Brett Lifestyle Portraits in Hingham, Massachusetts. Her work has appeared in many publications, including *New York* magazine, *The Boston Globe Magazine*, *Professional Photographer* magazine, and *Rangefinder* magazine. She was also a contributing photographer for *The Boston Globe* for six years, where she worked for her father. The quality of Kerry's work is frequently recognized; she has received her industry's top honors, including numerous Kodak Gallery Awards, Fuji Masterpiece Awards, and Courts of Honor. Kerry has a degree in art from the University of Massachusetts Boston. She is also a Master Photographer and Certified Professional Photographer through Professional Photographers of America. She lives in Hingham with her daughter, Morgan.

Carol Beggy is an award-winning writer and editor who has worked at several Eastern Massachusetts publications, including *The Boston Globe*, where she worked for more than 10 years. This is the fourth book she has worked on with Bill Brett. The coauthor of *101 Things I Hate About Your House*, Carol is a senior consultant to Saragoni & Company and a story producer/writer for local TV shows. A *cum laude* graduate of Northeastern University in Boston, she lives in Arlington, Massachusetts.

Karen Kaplan (see page 55) is president of Hill Holliday, the 17th largest advertising agency in the United States and the largest in New England. In 2008 she was elected president of the Massachusetts Women's Forum, a chapter of the International Women's Forum, a nonpolitical organization of preeminent women leaders worldwide. She lives in Marblehead, Massachusetts.

MARIA menounos

You might have seen **Maria Menounos** and her eye-catching gown on the red carpet at the Academy Awards as part of the official ABC preshow broadcast, or caught a glimpse of the *Access Hollywood* special correspondent at the Super Bowl. Or perhaps you heard Maria cheering for her beloved Boston Celtics during a playoff run, even if you weren't inside the TD Garden. A die-hard fan of all things related to Boston and its pro sports teams, Maria is a Medford native and alumna of the city's public high school. She attended Emerson College with her eyes set squarely on the prize of being a national television reporter. And succeed she did. Among Maria's many accomplishments: she was the youngest cohost of *Entertainment Tonight*, the youngest cohost of the *Today* show, and the youngest person to report for NBC's *Nightly News*. A former Miss Massachusetts Teen USA, Maria started her own charity, Take Action Hollywood!, which enlists celebrities to work for social change. She has also racked up an impressive list of acting and producing credits for television and movie projects, including the feature film *Serial Buddies*, which was shot in the Boston area in 2009. Her first book, *The EveryGirl's Guide to Life*, was released in April 2011 and quickly landed on *The New York Times'* best-sellers list.

SHANNON cook

Union members of Ironworkers Local 7, like **Shannon Cook**, often work at towering heights when erecting the metal structures of buildings and rigging cables on bridges. That a woman is a highly respected ironworker may surprise some, but Shannon's family and colleagues know that her calling is in her blood. She is a third-generation member of the storied Local 7 in South Boston, which began in 1896 as the International Association of Bridge, Structural and Ornamental Ironworkers. Her maternal grandfather, Hugh Bradley, was a member of the union, followed by his sons Alen and Jack Bradley, who helped get Shannon's father, Larry Cook, into the union in 1969. Her brother Sean and sister Ryan are also following in the family trade, as is Shannon's husband, Scott Queen. Shannon has two children, Aaron Cook and Charlotte Queen. She was the 2005 Apprentice of the Year and is now a foreman, a rarity for a woman. And when the time came for "topping out"—or placing the last structural beam on— the W Hotel in Boston, it was Shannon who was given the coveted honor, which was captured here by Bill Brett. When asked to share the toughest part of her job, Shannon said, "It's not the heights, it's the weather. I'd rather do a 50-story building than work through the winter along the Charles River."

CHRISTINE
coombs

Christine Coombs is still angry that her husband, Jeff, was killed on 9/11 while flying on Flight 11. But she said she decided early on "to take the grief and fear and turn it into positive energy to make a difference in my community and across Massachusetts and teach my kids to pay it forward." Christine and her three children—Matthew, Meaghan, and Julia—and their extended family and friends created the Jeffrey Coombs Memorial Foundation. And as the wars in Iraq and Afghanistan continued, the foundation began to extend support to military families, hosting an annual holiday party and other special programs for them. Two months after that fateful September morning, Christine and her family raised $50,000 through a yard sale and auction to help other 9/11 families in Massachusetts and New York. An Arizona transplant, and the youngest of 12 children, Christine is a former public relations professional who now donates services to a variety of nonprofits. In addition to being the president and founder of the Jeffrey Coombs Memorial Foundation, she is cochair of the Mass 9/11 Fund family advisory committee and a board member of several organizations, including the Massachusetts Military Heroes Fund, American Red Cross Blood Services in Massachusetts, and Congressman Bill Keating's Veterans' Advisory Board.

LINDA
pizzuti henry

Proud of her local roots and dedicated to making Boston a world-class city, **Linda Pizzuti Henry** has an extensive background in real estate and has worked for more than 10 years specializing in energy efficient development and urban infill projects. After receiving a bachelor of science degree from Babson College, Linda went on to earn a master's degree from the Center for Real Estate at the Massachusetts Institute of Technology. She is a director of both the Red Sox Foundation and the John W. Henry Family Foundation (named for her husband), which supports many charitable, educational, and cultural organizations and initiates innovative programs throughout Boston, New England, and Florida. This civically minded mom, who serves on the advisory board of the Boston Public Market, is actively involved in efforts to open a year-round local food market in Boston. To highlight the inspiring lives and charitable work of others, Linda cocreated Nacho Mama Productions, which produces the television show *After The Game* on NESN, featuring sports figures who have worked hard, lived well, and given back to their communities.

FREDERICA williams

In the nine years that **Frederica M. Williams** has been CEO and president of the Whittier Street Health Center, the number of people served at the Roxbury clinic has increased from 5,000 to 14,500. But she isn't stopping there. The goal for Whittier, which provides comprehensive health services regardless of a patient's ability to pay, is to grow the client roster to 24,000 through a new 78,000-square-foot addition that is expected to open in 2012. And it's not just the center that's getting notice; Frederica was named Outstanding Massachusetts Health Center Executive Director in 2010, and the Massachusetts Medical Society honored her with the organization's first Men's Health Award. After growing up in Sierra Leone, Frederica was educated at the London School of Accountancy, received an MBA from Anna Maria College, and earned a graduate certificate in administration and management from the Harvard Extension School. She worked at Dimock Community Health Center, Partners Healthcare, and Children's Hospital Boston before taking over the helm of Whittier in 2002. Frederica described her simple philosophy to a reporter: "I am here to be a servant leader."

MARY muse

Few people lead extraordinary lives, and fewer still have had their work and deeds read into the Congressional Record. In 2003, when retired Probate and Family Court Judge **Mary Beatty Muse** received a Lifetime Achievement Award from Boston College Law School (which she attended 50 years earlier), this daughter of Irish immigrants was recognized by the 108th Congress. An alumna of Boston Latin School for Girls and a 1941 graduate of Emmanuel College, Mary joined the Navy shortly after the bombing of Pearl Harbor, becoming part of the first class of the women's reserves (WAVES). After the war she attended Boston College Law School on the "GI Bill," graduating as one of three women in a class of some 160 students. Mary and her husband of nearly seven decades, Bob Muse—a noted trial lawyer and a decorated Marine Corps fighter pilot—have 11 children. A longtime supporter of professional and alumni groups, Mary is also active in Catholic Church affairs. In 1983 Mary was appointed a justice of the Massachusetts Trial Court. On the bench she was known for her firm but kindly manner. She remained on the Superior Court bench until her mandated retirement at the age of 70.

LINDA sloane kay | BARBARA sloane

For **Barbara J. G. Sloane**, right, and her daughter **Linda Sloane Kay**, Century Bank is a family affair. Wife of the bank's founder and chairman, Marshall M. Sloane, Barbara is a mother of three and grandmother to nine, and she once worked as a customer service representative in Century's Burlington branch. Linda, a wife and mother of two, is the bank's senior vice president and a member of the management committee. While Century, the largest family-controlled bank in New England, has prospered, both mother and daughter have been active in the community and committed to numerous philanthropic causes. Barbara has made important contributions to Boston University, Massachusetts General Hospital, Temple Israel, and the Boy Scouts of America. She is also a Lady Olave Baden-Powell Fellow, a high honor in the World Scout Foundation. Linda is an overseer at Boston University, the president of the Newton-Needham Chamber of Commerce, and was the cochair of the Special Olympics Massachusetts 2010 Gala.

17

AYLA brown | ARIANNA brown

They are best known as the daughters of U.S. Senator Scott Brown (who won the seat held for decades by the late Senator Edward M. Kennedy) and former WCVB-TV reporter Gail Huff, but **Ayla Brown**, left, and her younger sister, **Arianna Brown**, both have their own public successes— despite their youth. Ayla is a Boston College graduate where she was a standout basketball player. She became a household name in 2006 (while her father was a state senator) when she was a finalist on the Fox television show *American Idol*. She works as a special contributor for CBS's *The Early Show* and writes and produces country music, working out of Nashville. A premed student at Syracuse University, Arianna had a 4.0 grade point average at the end of her sophomore year. A part-time model for Maggie Trichon's Maggie Inc. agency, Arianna has modeled for Boston-based designer Michael De Paulo. After graduation, Arianna plans to pursue a career as an equine veterinarian. Arianna's plans don't surprise those who know her well. "She lives and breathes horses," said Gail of her younger daughter.

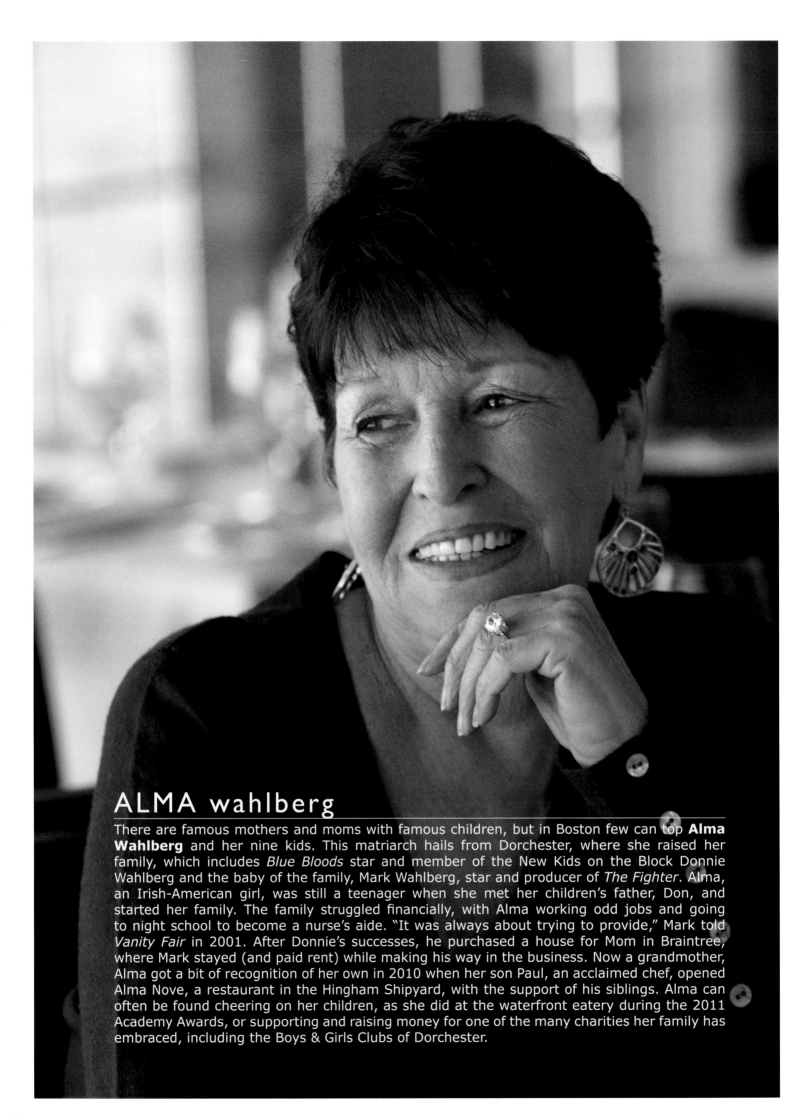

ALMA wahlberg

There are famous mothers and moms with famous children, but in Boston few can top **Alma Wahlberg** and her nine kids. This matriarch hails from Dorchester, where she raised her family, which includes *Blue Bloods* star and member of the New Kids on the Block Donnie Wahlberg and the baby of the family, Mark Wahlberg, star and producer of *The Fighter*. Alma, an Irish-American girl, was still a teenager when she met her children's father, Don, and started her family. The family struggled financially, with Alma working odd jobs and going to night school to become a nurse's aide. "It was always about trying to provide," Mark told *Vanity Fair* in 2001. After Donnie's successes, he purchased a house for Mom in Braintree, where Mark stayed (and paid rent) while making his way in the business. Now a grandmother, Alma got a bit of recognition of her own in 2010 when her son Paul, an acclaimed chef, opened Alma Nove, a restaurant in the Hingham Shipyard, with the support of his siblings. Alma can often be found cheering on her children, as she did at the waterfront eatery during the 2011 Academy Awards, or supporting and raising money for one of the many charities her family has embraced, including the Boys & Girls Clubs of Dorchester.

GAIL deegan

Gail Deegan knows her way around the business world and has carved out a record of attainment in corporate boardrooms. Gail served as the chief financial officer of three companies in different industries, including acting as CFO and executive vice president of textbook publishing giant Houghton Mifflin Company from 1996 until her retirement in 2001. Gail is a member of the board of directors of EMC Corporation and was previously a director of the TJX Companies, where she was chair of the audit committee and a member of the finance committee. Gail is much more than a numbers-cruncher. With a degree in education from The College of St. Rose, she worked as a teacher in Massachusetts and California. She received a master's degree in history from Ohio State University and earned an MBA from Simmons College School of Management, where she later would be an executive-in-residence. Among the many organizations Gail supports are United Way of Massachusetts Bay and Merrimack Valley, the Woods Hole Oceanographic Institute, and the Patriot's Trail Girl Scouts Council.

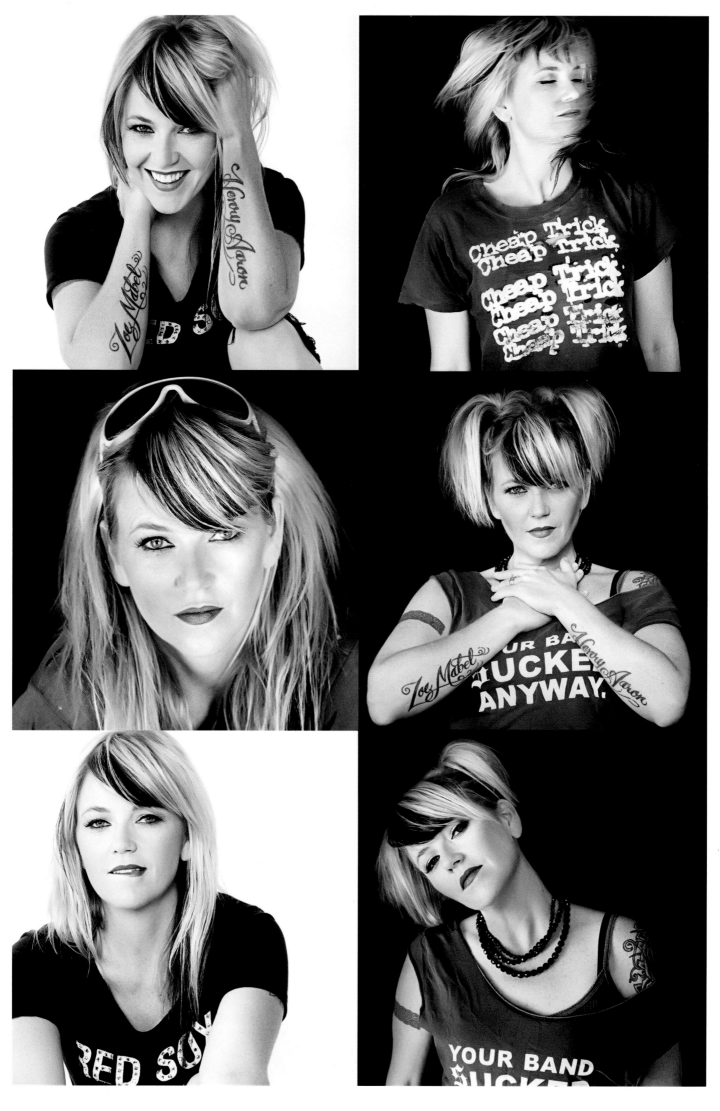

KAY hanley

You probably know her voice and have likely seen **Kay Hanley** in one of her many appearances in movies and on TV shows—or even as a backup singer on the national tour for Miley Cyrus. In her more than 20 years as a singer, songwriter, and musician, Kay has tallied a remarkable list of achievements, logged thousands of miles on tours, played hundreds of concerts—and she's showing no signs of slowing down. A near-perennial winner at the Boston Music Awards, this Dorchester native is best known for her years as the lead singer of the 1990s rock band Letters to Cleo, which included her husband, Michael Eisenstein. The couple has two children, Zoe Mabel and Henry Aaron—named for the ballplayer. (You can see their names tattooed on mom's forearms.) A die-hard baseball fan, particularly of the Red Sox, Kay is a regular in the lineup for the twice-annual Hot Stove, Cool Music charity concert hosted by Red Sox General Manager Theo Epstein and Hall of Fame baseball journalist Peter Gammons. Kay is a favorite of New England Patriots fans because the team has won nearly every time Kay has sung the national anthem. After a solo career and releasing three albums, Kay's latest project is the band Palmdale.

ENITH levine | NANCY schneider

This may look like a high-end Newbury Street boutique, but, in fact, it is the Boston headquarters of Dress for Success. The Boston branch of the nonprofit organization has helped more than 6,000 women since it was founded in 2001 by **Enith Levine**, left, and **Nancy Schneider**. The mission of Dress for Success is to promote the economic independence of disadvantaged women by providing them with professional attire and a network of support and career development tools to help them succeed in work and in life. Before opening the Boston location of Dress for Success, Enith enjoyed an accomplished career in both architecture and interior design, developing, designing, and building projects for more than 30 years. Her interests extend to the arts, and for many years she taught dance and drama for emotionally-challenged adolescents. Nancy is a freelance writer and social worker. She has worked extensively with battered women and said she knows that economic freedom can be powerful: "The women I saw escape from abuse did so because they believed they could make it on their own. With confidence and economic independence, I believe women will make the right choices for their children."

MARIAN mcgovern

The Massachusetts State Police that Colonel **Marian J. McGovern** runs today is a much different agency than the one she joined as a freshly minted trooper three decades ago. Then there were fewer than 10 female state troopers, while today women make up almost a tenth of the force. Marian took the oath of office on January 14, 2010, as the superintendent of the State Police, becoming the first woman commander of the department. Marian and her department were tested early in her tenure with several high-profile cases and tragedies. She was up for the challenge. Marian began at the State Police as a road trooper in 1979 before becoming a detective and then commander of the Worcester County State Police Detective Unit. As a major, she was assigned to the crime lab, where she helped develop the unit that enters DNA evidence into a national database. She oversaw the state's implementation of the AMBER Alert program, which is activated to find abducted children. As a lieutenant colonel, she served as commander of the Division of Standards and Training, which oversees internal investigations and the State Police Academy. And in January 2009 she was appointed deputy superintendent, the department's second-in-command.

MAUREEN dunn

Long after others would have given up, **Maureen Dunn** soldiers on in her efforts to ensure that those who serve in the U.S. military and their families don't ever endure the same difficulties she faced nearly four decades ago. Maureen was living her own version of the American dream in the early 1960s when, as a young newlywed, her dashing husband, Joe Dunn, enlisted in the Navy, attended flight school, and volunteered to serve in Vietnam. On Valentine's Day, 1968— 11 days after his first tour of duty was extended—Lieutenant Joe Dunn was piloting his jet, with the call sign *Canasta* 404, when he drifted into Chinese airspace and was shot down. Maureen, who was raising their then-19-month-old son, Joe Jr., began her odyssey to find answers as to what happened to her husband, who was promoted to commander after he was declared MIA. Accounts suggested Joe might have survived the initial attack, but Maureen, determined to prove her husband was still alive, was met with resistance from the U.S. government. She responded by organizing the "Where is Lt. Joe Dunn?" committee, one of the first POW/MIA activist organizations in the country. Her activism continues today, but most of all she keeps alive the memory of her husband, who is among the more than 1,800 still unaccounted for. Maureen's portrait was taken in the hallway of her Randolph home holding a copy of *The Search for* Canasta *404: Love, Loss, and the POW/MIA Movement*, a book Maureen wrote with former Associated Press reporter Melissa B. Robinson.

GRETCHEN monahan

Boston may not be the most likely place to start a successful career in the fashion world, but **Gretchen Monahan**'s journey to the great runways of the world began just a bit west of the city in Waltham. While working in the café of Yolanda Cellucci's now-closed Yolanda's salon and spa, Gretta (a nickname given to Gretchen by her grandfather) had a front-row seat to a perpetual fashion show. Raised in Cambridge and Waltham, Gretta attended the Fashion Institute of Technology in New York City but decided to return home and train as a master colorist. She opened her first salon in Wellesley, Massachusetts, when she was 24, and now her GrettaStyle brand includes fashion and accessory lines, the Grettacole salons, GSpas, and Grettaluxe boutiques. Since the birth of Kai Rei, her son with actor Ricky Paull Goldin, Gretta divides her time between Los Angeles, New York, and Boston. Already enjoying success as a stylist, Gretta became nationally known when she started styling Rachael Ray (see page 69) and appearing on her show. Gretta then had a personal goal come true when she got to work with fashion authority Tim Gunn on his TV show *Guide to Style*. Gretta uses her success and new outlets to promote various charitable causes, such as Boston's Faulkner Hospital and New York's North Shore Animal League America.

KATHLEEN driscoll

Kathleen F. Driscoll is the first person to give credit to those who have helped support the capital projects of the Roman Catholic Archdiocese of Boston and the schools and programs run by the church in the Boston area. So you'd have to ask others just how important this humble, busy mom of six has been to those efforts. In 2010 the Boston College alumna was named the secretary for institutional advancement and the chief development officer for the archdiocese by Cardinal Seán P. O'Malley, and she also serves on the Cardinal's cabinet. A respected and successful marketing, communications, and development professional, Kathleen has been the president of the Campaign for Catholic Schools since 2008. (The CCS operates as a donor-advised fund and has raised more than $58 million for four schools—Trinity Catholic Academy in Brockton, Pope John Paul II Catholic Academy in Dorchester/Mattapan, St. Ann School in Gloucester, and South Boston Catholic Academy.) She previously worked at John Hancock Financial Services and Hill Holiday. Kathleen is a member of Women Affirming Life and serves on the boards of Catholic Charities and Pope John Paul II Catholic Academy. In 2011 she cochaired a Priest Appreciation Dinner that raised $1 million.

LAURA sen

BJ's Wholesale Club Chief Executive Officer **Laura J. Sen** spent most of 2010 and 2011 refocusing the Natick-based company to better suit the needs of its customers. She knows what customers want because she herself shops at BJ's. Her hands-on approach has not gone unnoticed. In late 2008, when the news alert hit the business tracking websites that Laura, BJ's president and chief operating officer, had been named the company's chief executive officer, it caused hardly a ripple on Wall Street. That's because the 30-year veteran of retailing was seen not only as the heir apparent to the membership warehouse company's top post, but also as the best person to lead the company back to prominence in the tough wholesale retailing market. Laura knows BJ's well, having worked from 1997 to 2003 as executive vice president of merchandising and logistics, a position she returned to in 2007 after running her own retail consulting company for a few years. In 2010 Laura was the only female among the 14 business leaders of major locally-based companies that had formed the Massachusetts Competitive Partnership, which advocates for the state to create jobs through economic development policies.

FRANCES rivera

Just as media pundits were proclaiming that the era of the television news anchor was over, along came **Frances Rivera**, who continues to be a ratings winner and a favorite among viewers. Frances grew up in Dallas, and she credits her Filipino heritage as the source of her adventurous spirit and dedication to community. She received her bachelor's degree in journalism from the University of the Philippines and joined 7News/WHDH-TV in 2001. In July 2011 Frances announced she was leaving Boston to head to New York where she will anchor WPIX-TV's morning news. She said that although she welcomed the change in schedule it was hard to leave Boston, where she coanchored, with Kim Khazei, four nightly newscasts for the NBC affiliate. Frances won Emmy Awards from the National Academy of Television Arts and Sciences/New England for her work at the Channel 7 anchor desk. An avowed foodie, she hosted a segment on WHDH called "The Dish," which featured some of Boston's best-known chefs and their culinary secrets. She was also a regular fixture on Boston's charity circuit. In 2010, Frances and her husband, Stuart Fraass, welcomed their first child, a daughter, Tessa.

SHANNON allen

While the Boston Celtics acquired an outstanding three-point shooter in the 2007 trade for Ray Allen, the city of Boston also got one of its most dogged fund-raisers and energetic personalities with the arrival of his wife, **Shannon Allen**. The trade meant a homecoming of sorts for this Connecticut-born singer, songwriter, and actress, who studied for a music business degree at Northeastern University before pursuing her dream of performing. It didn't take long after graduating for Shannon to get noticed. She was part of the Shades, which recorded on the Motown label, and later focused on acting, landing several stage roles and parts on the HBO hit *Sex and the City* and in *Girlfight*, which won the Grand Jury Award at the Sundance Film Festival. Shannon has been a regular on the local and national fund-raising scene supporting a variety of projects. But it was when son Walker, the third of Ray and Shannon's four children (Tierra, Ray III, and Wynn are the others) was diagnosed with Type 1 diabetes during the 2008 NBA Finals that she became a national face for finding a cure. Shannon continues to work in the music business with the independent record label she coowns and operates, Superstar Music Group. In early 2011 Shannon and Ray launched *The Pre-Game Meal*, a 30-minute television show on NECN and Comcast SportsNet that features Shannon cooking with Boston's sports figures and others of note.

MARINA kalb

Marina Kalb's childhood was spent in Hong Kong, overlooking the South China Sea. Her earliest memories are of creating a shop in her life-size dollhouse, complete with a selection of used shoes and her favorite clothes. It's no surprise that she has recreated the same approach through her partnership with Kristina Hare Lyons (see opposite page) on Portobello Road, the lifestyle boutique they opened in 2008 that is filled with finds from around the world, including jewelry from Turkey, clothing from Europe and Asia, linens from India, sweets and jams from France, and fresh flowers from Holland. Although it may seem like a world away from her 20-year career in documentary journalism, Marina sees the experiences through a single lens: capturing a wonderful story, be it chasing the president, as she did numerous times for work on documentaries for the PBS series *Frontline*, or finding the perfect piece of handcrafted jewelry. The daughter of the eminent journalist Bernard Kalb, Marina travels the world on the lookout for new and fresh things that she can take home as mementos. Her motto: "Style is all about what's on the inside, though it doesn't hurt to look damn good at the same time."

KRISTINA
hare lyons

Kristina Hare Lyons is a successful businesswoman and mom-on-the-go, who manages to navigate her busy life with a sense of style. Kristina coowns, with her best friend Marina Kalb (see opposite page), Portobello Road, a lifestyle boutique in Chestnut Hill featuring a carefully edited selection of clothing, accessories, jewelry, and gifts from all over the world, as well as fresh flowers. Her professional highlights include her coordination of a landmark study with the United Nations for Physicians for Human Rights on war-related sexual violence in Sierra Leone. Kristina was an associate producer at *Frontline*, where she met Marina, and West Coast editor of *Elle* magazine. Kristina also worked as an assistant to Oliver Stone on three of his most notable films: *Born on the Fourth of July*, *The Doors*, and *JFK*. She received her bachelor of arts degree from Tufts University and a master's degree from the Fletcher School of Law and Diplomacy. After graduation, Kristina followed her dear friend Vanessa Kirsch onto the campaign trail for then-Massachusetts Governor Michael Dukakis' presidential campaign. Kristina and her husband, Patrick Lyons, Boston's legendary restaurant and entertainment entrepreneur, have two children. She splits her time between Brookline and Martha's Vineyard. She is developing a feature film based on Jenna Blum's best-selling novel *Those Who Save Us*.

BEVERLY edgehill

Beverly Edgehill has dedicated her professional life to identifying, nurturing, and training emerging business leaders and is CEO and president of The Partnership, Inc., a nonprofit leadership development and career-mentoring organization for multicultural professionals. More than 2,000 professionals of color and 250 leading corporations have used the services of The Partnership. Beverly is a graduate of Teachers College at Columbia University and has a doctorate in leadership and organizational learning. Her research is focused on how professional women learn to have career success. She is a strategic advisor to corporations and a mentor to individuals, covering everything from Fortune 500 companies to small nonprofits. Prior to founding her own leadership and organization development practice, she was vice president for leadership and organization development at Fidelity Investments from 1993 to 2005. She is a columnist for *Color Magazine*, serves on the board of trustees at Beth Israel Deaconess Medical Center and on the strategic advisory board for Simmons School of Management. She is also on the boards of the Greater Boston Chamber of Commerce, Beaver Country Day School, and The Commonwealth Institute. To top it all off, Beverly is a New England selection panelist for The White House Fellows program.

CAROL sawyer parks

Even as she sits in her aerie overseeing the work of Sawyer Enterprises, **Carol Sawyer Parks** has her feet firmly planted on the ground. The daughter of Frank Sawyer, former owner of Checker Taxi Co. (you can see his hat on her desk), Carol is the first woman to develop a high-rise tower in Boston: the W Boston Hotel and Residences, which comprises 235 hotel rooms, a spa, restaurants, and other amenities on the first 15 floors, and 123 condominiums on the upper 13 floors. Opened in 2009 at the corner of Stuart and Tremont streets (a space that for years featured a parking lot and a hole in the ground), the W, with its glass and metal façade, cuts a stunning profile in the city's theater district. Like many developers, Carol has not always been without controversy, but she doesn't shy away from a challenge. She counts the swanky Niketown building on Newbury Street at Exeter Street among her early successes. With her trademark white hair, she has landed on *The Boston Globe*'s "25 Most Stylish Bostonians" list. A trustee of Suffolk University, Carol has been a supporter of a number of local charities, including Floating Hospital for Children's Cancer Center, Rosie's Place, and The Home for Little Wanderers.

JENNIFER clarke

She is an in-demand commercial fishing captain, a world-class angler, and a successful singer-songwriter. All of which means **Jennifer Clarke** doesn't easily fit in to any one category. But on Martha's Vineyard, where people thrive by juggling several careers, she fits right in. Jen is married to actor-comedian Lenny Clarke, (who ably served as Kerry Brett's photography assistant, making sure Kerry didn't fall off the boat as Jen's portrait was taken). As can be seen in this photograph with the Gay Head Cliffs in the background, Jen takes great comfort from and is fully at ease on the water. She runs Captain Clarke Charters out of Menemsha and is often booked for trips months in advance. Jen got her start fishing as a four year old in the freshwater streams of the Shenandoah Valley. A native of Delaplane, Virginia, Jen comes from a family of avid trout fly fishermen and has tested her angling skills around the world. Her Virginia roots have also played a role in developing Jen's musical style. She has worked as a songwriter in Nashville, where part of her *More Than I Have* album was recorded. *Mr. Pain*, a track from that release, was used in actor-comedian (and friend) Denis Leary's FX series *Rescue Me*.

ROSEANNA means

When Dr. **Roseanna H. Means** was an internist working with Boston's homeless population, she couldn't help but notice that women and children did not have access to the level of care they needed. As she graduated from the Tufts University School of Medicine and got her training at Brigham and Women's Hospital, she came to know the city well and the people who live on its streets. After 10 years of working with the homeless, she founded Women of Means in 1999, a not-for-profit organization that offers direct, free medical care to thousands of homeless women and children. Her mission, and that of her nonprofit, is "to improve the lives of women who are homeless or marginally housed through quality health care, education, and advocacy." Each year a team of 20 volunteer and paid medical professionals provides more than $500,000 in services through Women of Means, a model program that has been recognized nationally. But for Roseanna it is not about the health care alone; it is about providing a safe place for women and children. "The women come into the shelters to get warm, to eat, to feel safe. And we're already there," she said in an interview with CNN.

TRACY campion

Within the first few years of launching her own company, Boston real estate broker **Tracy Campion** oversaw more than $531 million in sales of residential properties. Any survey of the most coveted Boston properties on the market reveals several Campion & Co. listings. To put that staggering success into perspective, this leading Back Bay broker has sold more properties than the entire value of some small Midwestern towns. How does she continually land the most desirable listings and count some of the city's most influential property owners, developers, and institutions among her clients? Simply, they trust her, a confidence she earned over the years, particularly during her tenure at R. M. Bradley & Company's real estate division, where she was senior vice president and manager before she left to found her own firm. This Emmanuel College alumna is a ubiquitous fixture on the local charity and civic circuit.

LYDIA shire

Lydia Shire can't remember a time when food, cooking, and being in a kitchen weren't part of her life. One of the pillars of Boston's food community, Lydia has a few establishments where diners can sample her trademark fare: Scampo in The Liberty Hotel, the historic downtown eatery Locke-Ober, Blue Sky at the Atlantic House Hotel on York Beach, Maine, and her latest, Towne Stove and Spirits, with Jasper White and The Lyons Group. A Brookline native who was raised by artist parents, Lydia's earliest memories are of peeling garlic alongside her father. After cooking as a young wife and mother, Lydia began working her way up the ranks as a "salad girl," slicing paté and shucking oysters, at the venerable (but now closed) Maison Robert. After studying at Le Cordon Bleu cooking school in London, Lydia returned to Maison Robert as a line cook and, later, head chef. Her string of successes in Boston includes Harvest, Café Plaza, Parker's, Seasons, BIBA, and Excelsior. And in 1986 she opened the Four Seasons Hotel in Beverly Hills, becoming the first female executive chef to open a luxury property for the Four Seasons Hotels & Resorts Company.

CARMEN ortiz

As the state's federal prosecutor, **Carmen M. Ortiz** knows the importance of her job and the symbolism of what she represents. "Being the first woman and first Hispanic U.S. attorney in Massachusetts is not lost on me," Carmen said at her swearing-in ceremony in January 2010, after just a few months on the job. Carmen comes from a humble background, growing up in New York City's Spanish Harlem neighborhood as the oldest of five children. Her family later moved to Long Island, where Carmen graduated from Adelphi University. She earned a full scholarship to George Washington Law School in Washington, D.C., and, after her graduation in 1981 she started making her mark in the legal world. Carmen worked at Harvard Law School and was a prosecutor in the Middlesex District Attorney's office. She was an assistant U.S. attorney in the Boston office for 12 years in the Economic Crimes Unit before her appointment as U.S. attorney. Recommended for her job by the state's U.S. senators, Carmen said it was the late Senator Edward M. Kennedy who informed her of her nomination. "I told Senator Kennedy that, if confirmed, I would make him proud," Carmen told *The Boston Globe*. "And I intend to honor his legacy."

SANDRA edgerley

Sandra M. Edgerley's commitment to family extends beyond her husband, Paul, her four children, and her parents. With a Harvard undergraduate degree and an MBA from the Harvard Business School, Sandy set out on a successful career in business strategy consulting for Bain and Company. The Brookline resident—shown here in the home she has opened for Boston charities—has focused her energy and business savvy on working with nonprofit organizations, particularly those that help families and children. Sandy has been most involved with the Boys & Girls Clubs of Boston: She has chaired the board of directors for five years and has been a director for 12 years, during which time she helped complete a $100-million capital campaign. Sandy also has been committed to the United Way of Massachusetts Bay and Merrimack Valley, cochairing the Tocqueville Society for more than 10 years and helping to spearhead a middle school violence prevention program called Out of Harm's Way. The nonprofits Horizons for Homeless Children, Be The Change, and The Boston Foundation are also close to Sandy's heart.

ELAINE schuster

Elaine Schuster is a philanthropist, civic activist, and health care and education advocate. A mother and grandmother, in 2009 Elaine was appointed by President Obama as a public delegate to the General Assembly of the United Nations, where she focused her work on the area of human trafficking. Elaine and her husband, Gerald, were given the 2002 Heritage Award from Brigham and Women's Hospital, where she serves on the Trust Board and the Women's Health Forum. The couple founded the Brandeis Center for Investigative Journalism at Brandeis University, where she is a board member of the Women's Research Program. She has worked on behalf of (and served on the boards of) numerous organizations, including the Franciscan Children's Hospital, Harvard Medical School, the former Wang Center for the Performing Arts, Suffolk University, and the Boston Public Library Foundation. She is also a cofounder of PEACE, one of the nation's leading community-based network centers that provides mentoring, tutoring, and life skills training for inner-city children. Splitting her time between Brookline and Palm Beach, Florida, Elaine is among the most prominent fund-raisers for the Democratic Party. A board member of the White House Project, she is a managing trustee of the Democratic National Committee.

CALLIE crossley

Media commentator and radio show host **Callie Crossley** loves the stories behind the stories. Callie has been called a "woman of all media," not just for her willingness to adapt to the changing technical landscape, but also for her work in traditional journalism. She is the host of an eponymous one-hour, weekday issues radio show that was part of WGBH-FM's 2010 relaunch and is a regular commentator on *Greater Boston* weekly media review "Beat the Press" on WGBH-TV. She was nominated for an Academy Award and won an Emmy Award for her work on the 1987 documentary feature *Eyes on the Prize: America's Civil Rights Years, Bridge to Freedom 1965*. Callie was also a producer for the ABC News program *20/20* focusing on health issues. A graduate of Wellesley College, she was a Nieman Fellow at Harvard University. A frequent lecturer and commentator, Callie is a Woodrow Wilson Visiting Fellow and has served as program manager for the Nieman Foundation for Journalism at Harvard, directing the speakers program. Off the air, Callie is known as an oenophile, regularly writing about wine on her blog, "The Crushed Grape Report."

DEB samuels

Deb Samuels, executive director of Crossroads for Kids, doesn't just run camp programs for young people—she lives and breathes them. On the Duxbury-based not-for-profit's website, Deb states that her favorite camp activity is "camp songs—anyplace anytime!" Crossroads for Kids runs traditional summer programs at camps in Massachusetts, but its programs don't end by Labor Day. At-risk young people enter the Crossroads for Kids 10-year program with their first summer of camp, transition into year-round programming via the Camper Continuity Initiative, and then graduate to the C5 Teen program in the 8th grade. Since joining Crossroads for Kids in 2001 as the director of Camp Wing in Duxbury, Deb has come to know the organization from the ground up. She later became director of Crossroads' Camp Lapham in Ashby, Massachusetts, and is now the founding director of Crossroads' C5 New England Teen Leadership Program, which combines immersive summer programs with year-round mentoring. A graduate of University of Technology, Sydney (Australia), Deb was named executive director of Crossroads in April 2006.

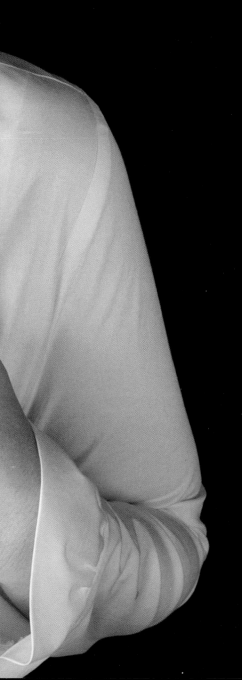

KELLEY tuthill

Kelley Tuthill is a journalist's journalist. A reporter with WCVB-TV since 1998, Kelley has become a familiar and trusted newswoman, covering hundreds of stories from the lightest feature to the hardest news. In June 2011 Kelley scored a national exclusive when she obtained from a law enforcement source the first photo taken of fugitive James "Whitey" Bulger and his girlfriend Catherine Greig after their capture. Other major stories Kelley has covered include the deadly tornadoes that ripped through Central and Western Massachusetts in 2011, the *Columbia* space shuttle explosion, the 2004 Red Sox World Series championship run, and the Patriots' first Super Bowl victory. A breast cancer survivor, Kelley broke an old rule of journalism and allowed herself to become the story. She covered her diagnosis, surgery, chemotherapy, radiation, and life after cancer and kept a video diary on the station's website. Kelley and her friend Elisha Daniels (see page 123) coauthored *You Can Do This! Surviving Breast Cancer Without Losing Your Sanity or Your Style*. Today this mother of two daughters is one of Boston's most effective fund-raisers for breast cancer research and care. The annual Kelley for Ellie fashion show, created by WCVB-TV anchor Susan Wornick and others to honor Kelley, raises thousands of dollars for the Ellie Fund's mission of helping breast cancer patients and their families.

DOROTHY aufiero

Dorothy Aufiero built her career at a time when her industry didn't really exist in Boston. When Dot graduated from Emerson College, her contemporaries who dreamed of making it in film and television production moved west to Los Angeles. She, however, took a job at WSBK-TV38 in the sales department and volunteered in production, her true interest, whenever she could. She later did the same thing at WCVB-TV, where she was a cofounder of Studio 5 Productions (a division of the ABC affiliate). After a few years, the world of filmmaking called and Dot gave up a steady paycheck, got herself into IATSE Local 161, and landed her first job on a movie, doing "pick-up shots" in New York for the Tom Hanks movie *Joe Versus the Volcano*. Dot worked on most of the few movies that were filmed in Boston while spending the majority of her professional time in New York. She later worked on *The Good Son* with David Collins and Michael Williams. The trio formed Scout Productions in 1994 and had a notable 10-year run producing movies and television shows before hitting it big in 2004 with *Queer Eye for the Straight Guy*. When Scout was at its peak, Dot sold her stake in the company to once again follow her heart and produce movies. And she did just that as the producer of the "Irish" Micky Ward story, *The Fighter*, starring Mark Wahlberg, which received a Best Picture Oscar nomination in 2011.

KAREN kaplan

Karen Kaplan is living proof that, with hard work and making the most of opportunities presented to you, you can achieve great success. Karen joined Hill Holliday, one of the country's preeminent advertising agencies, in 1982 as a receptionist—something to do before law school—and she never left. Nearly three decades later, she is president of Hill Holliday and ranks among Boston's most powerful women. She serves on the executive committee of the Greater Boston Chamber of Commerce, the board of governors of the Chief Executives' Club of Boston, the corporate board resource committee of The Boston Club, and the board of the Massachusetts Conference for Women and was elected president of the Massachusetts Women's Forum in 2008. Karen is also one of the city's most philanthropic citizens; she was the 2009 recipient of the Charles E. Rogerson Award for Community Service and has worked on behalf of too many city nonprofits to list.

DREW gilpin faust

The 28th president of Harvard University, **Drew Gilpin Faust** knows how significant it is that she is running the country's oldest college. "I hope that my own appointment can be one symbol of an opening of opportunities that would have been inconceivable even a generation ago," Drew said at a 2007 press conference announcing her selection. But, she added, "I'm not the woman president of Harvard, I'm the president of Harvard." She was ready for the challenge. Drew was the founding dean of the Radcliffe Institute for Advanced Study at Harvard, overseeing the transformation of the former women's college into an academic incubator and think tank. A noted historian of the Civil War and the American South, Drew is also Harvard's Lincoln Professor of History. The author of six books, Drew's *This Republic of Suffering: Death and the American Civil War* won the Bancroft Prize in 2009. Previously, she was a 25-year member of the faculty at the University of Pennsylvania, her alma mater. Drew grew up in Virginia's Shenandoah Valley, graduated from Concord Academy, received her bachelor's degree from Bryn Mawr College, and her master's and doctoral degrees from Penn. She is the first Harvard president since 1672 who did not receive an undergraduate or graduate degree from the university.

GRACE cyr

It is no exaggeration to say that **Grace Cyr**'s love knows no bounds. This Billerica woman, now 90, has cared for 93 foster children over the past 45 years. Grace and her husband, Frank, have opened their doors to children who were most in need of a place to stay. Several days a week, Grace gets up at 4:30 a.m. to bathe, dress, and feed Kayla, 20 (shown here with Grace), who has cerebral palsy and cannot walk or talk. Kayla has been in Grace's care for more than 15 years. Their photograph was taken at the 2010 annual fund-raiser for The Home for Little Wanderers, a child and family services agency that is the country's oldest and one of New England's largest. Grace was honored at the gala for her remarkable dedication; she is the nonprofit organization's longest-serving foster parent and the one who has cared for the most children. Grace has never given up on any of the children sent to her, even though many had serious emotional or physical problems. She began as a foster parent in 1966 at the suggestion of one of her five daughters (with her first husband, Gordon), who had become a foster parent herself. Grace said that when she was growing up in Charlestown her family couldn't afford to send her to nursing school. Still she found a way to live her dream and care for children.

MARILYN riseman

Marilyn Riseman *is* Boston fashion. With her trademark bob and seemingly over-the-top makeup, she is the embodiment of what great fashion aspires to: an authentic statement of timeless style. Now in her 80s, this grandmother is still a regular fixture on the social scene, sometimes logging several high-profile events in a week. (At any given gala, you might find a half-dozen people gathered to listen as Marilyn spins her often saucy yarns.) She got her start in the fashion business as a handbag buyer for a Boston department store. Later she opened her own boutique on Newbury Street that for many years was the local epicenter of the hottest trends in fashion. Marilyn regularly traveled to Europe for buying sprees to restock her store, often making deals with emerging designers who would become icons of fashion in the latter part of the 20th Century, including Giorgio Armani, Gianni Versace, and Roberto Cavalli. What many don't know about Marilyn is the depth of her local roots and how many people have been helped through her civic action and her family's philanthropy. She hosts a regular lunch series to promote the local fashion scene and eagerly throws her support behind the newest designers. "What's the point of leaving it all in your closet?" Marilyn asked. "People need to support the talents and the causes that matter to them. That's what I do."

ANGELA peri

Being on the receiving end of the e-mail blasts sent from **Angela Peri**'s Boston Casting means having a front-row seat to Boston's burgeoning television and film production industry. Whether working on a blockbuster drama starring Mark Wahlberg, a comedy starring Kevin James, or an open casting call for a nationally broadcast reality show, Angela plumbs the rosters of the region's residents, always looking for that perfect person to fill a role. The founder and owner of Boston Casting, Angela knows what it's like to be on the other side of the camera. A former actress and stand-up comedienne, she founded her agency in 1991 and has since worked on hundreds of local, regional, and national projects, from major motion pictures, including *The Fighter, Ted, Here Comes the Boom, Knight and Day, Pink Panther 2, The Game Plan, Paul Blart: Mall Cop, The Proposal,* and *Edge of Darkness*, to television shows, commercials, and corporate films. A member of the Casting Society of America, Angela was recognized by *Imagine* magazine in 2009 as one of the industry's innovators. She is an original board member of the Massachusetts Production Coalition. An active member of the community, she lends her expertise to organizations and events related to autism. She was the 2008 recipient of the Dr. Margaret L. Bauman Award, which is given annually to an outstanding local parent from the community dealing with autistic issues.

MARY finlay

If the important business of information technology is solely the province of men and stereotypical computer geeks, someone forgot to tell **Mary Finlay**. Mary is a professor at the Simmons School of Management, where she received a master's degree in business administration. She has been on the faculty of Simmons since 1985. The former deputy chief information officer of Partners HealthCare System, Mary oversaw the daily management of an organization of 1,300 information systems and telecommunications staff. Previously, she was the CIO at Brigham and Women's Hospital, which is part of Partners HealthCare. In addition to training the next generation of IT executives, Mary is active in Boston's high-tech community. She is a trustee of the Massachusetts Technology Leadership Council and has served as the council's chair. She is a board member of the Boston chapter of the Society of Information Management and a member of the Healthcare Information and Management Systems Society and the College of Healthcare Information Executives. Mary, whose first job out of Allegheny College was as a counselor in an adolescent group home in Erie, Pennsylvania, has been recognized with leadership awards from Simmons School of Management, the New England Business and Technology Association, and Babson College.

NIKI tsongas
THERESE murray
MARTHA coakley

Three of the state's top Democratic leaders enjoyed the welcome of a crowd on a night when their party had a lot to celebrate in December, 2009: Massachusetts Attorney General **Martha Coakley**, right, U.S. Representative **Niki Tsongas**, left, and State Senate President **Therese Murray**. Martha had won the Democratic primary for the U.S. Senate seat left vacant by the death of long-standing senator Edward M. Kennedy. Though she ultimately lost to Scott Brown in a special election, she has still rung up a number of accomplishments to applaud. A North Adams native, she is a distinguished prosecutor who was the Middlesex district attorney before being elected as the state's first female attorney general. When Niki was elected in 2007, she became the first woman from Massachusetts to serve in Congress in 25 years. Niki holds the same seat that her late husband, Paul Tsongas, who later became a U.S. senator and presidential candidate, held three decades earlier. Before entering politics, Niki raised her family, practiced law, and was a dean at Middlesex Community College. Therese also broke new barriers when she was elected to the top spot in the state Senate. A longtime resident of Plymouth, Terry has served as a community advocate and health activist. She has been involved with the Massachusetts Public Health Association, the Statewide Breast Cancer Advisory Board, and the Pilgrim Society. First elected to the state Senate in 1992, Terry was chair of the Senate Ways and Means Committee before being elected as Senate president.

TONYA mezrich

As a prominent fashionista and social figure in Boston, **Tonya Mezrich** has made quite the mark on the local scene in her time in Boston. Tonya's nonprofit work includes the Museum Council of the Museum of Fine Arts, the Animal Rescue League of Boston, and the Boston Ballet Young Partners Group, of which she is cochair. She also works with the Pet Pals program, bringing her trained therapy dog, Bugsy, for regular visits to the Susan Bailis Assisted Living Facility. Tonya launched Mike & Ton, a line of office-to-evening dresses she created with designer Michael De Paulo, in 2011. She is a nonpracticing dentist who also designs original jewelry using the skills she learned while studying at Tufts University's School of Dental Medicine. Mom to young Asher and the wife of *New York Times* best-selling author Ben Mezrich, Tonya has carved out her own media career doing "Tagged by Tonya" fashion segments for NECN's *The Morning Show* and working as a contributing editor at Niche Media's *Boston Common* magazine. In 2007 *The Boston Globe* listed Tonya as one of the top "25 Most Stylish Bostonians."

BARBARA lynch

For chef and restaurateur **Barbara Lynch**, opening three establishments in South Boston's Fort Point Channel neighborhood was a homecoming. And she came home with a flourish: Menton, Barbara's upscale French and Italian–inspired restaurant where Kerry Brett photographed this portrait, received a rare and coveted four-star review from *The Boston Globe*. This South Boston native got her first job at age 13, cooking at a local rectory. Winner of a James Beard Award for her skills in the kitchen, she worked with some of Boston's best-known chefs and restaurateurs before opening her first eatery, No. 9 Park, in 1998. The Beacon Hill restaurant immediately began racking up rave reviews and was named one of the "Top 25 New Restaurants in America" by *Bon Appétit* and "Best New Restaurant" by *Food & Wine*. As the CEO of Barbara Lynch Gruppo, Barbara oversees the operations of nine establishments, including B&G Oysters and The Butcher Shop in the South End, that employ more than 200 people. Each year this mom dedicates time and resources to a number of philanthropic missions, including The Crittenton Women's Union, Common Threads, The Greater Boston Food Bank, and Share Our Strength.

WENDY semonian eppich

Wendy Semonian Eppich got her corner office the hard way: climbing the ladder of the family business, from summer volunteer to chief executive. Most people think she has always been the publisher of *The Improper Bostonian*, a twice-monthly chronicle of Boston's who's who and what's what that was founded by her brother Mark Semonian 20 years ago. Wendy graduated from the University of Maine at Orono in December 1992 with a degree in international affairs, and during a summer break she helped her brother get out the first issue. Wendy truly began her career at the publication as a classified account executive and worked her way up to the positions of sales and marketing director and associate publisher before taking the reins. Her commitment to community extends beyond the magazine. This mother of two young boys is executive director of Leslie's Links, which honors the memory of her sister, Leslie, and has raised more than a million dollars for the Ewing's Sarcoma Fund at the Dana-Farber Cancer Institute. Leslie was a remarkable woman in her own right. First diagnosed with cancer in 1991, Leslie finally succumbed to the disease in 1999, but she packed a whole lot into that last decade, including earning an MBA and raising money for cancer research.

RACHAEL ray

Born into a family where food was the centerpiece of living, **Rachael Ray** spent time as a child in Mashpee and Falmouth on Cape Cod, where her family owned a restaurant called The Carvery. As a television show host, Rachael has made her name in the kitchen, but she'd be the first to correct you if you called her a chef. The queen of *30 Minute Meals* (that title became her trademark and the name of the first of her three Food Network shows), Rachael is known for using boxed ingredients, short cuts, and things found in regular homes rather than the well-stocked pantries of gourmet chefs. In 2007 The Oxford American College Dictionary added the term EVOO (an acronym for Extra Virgin Olive Oil), crediting Rachael with coining and popularizing the term as a word. In 2010 her eponymous syndicated daily show won a Daytime Emmy Award in the Best Talk Show category. Rachael is noted for giving a career boost to others, including stylist Gretchen Monahan (see page 28).

RACHEL dratch

Rachel Dratch is a fearless performer. The consummate comic actress, she throws herself, sometimes literally, into her roles. A graduate of Dartmouth College, Rachel is a Lexington native who made her name on *Saturday Night Live* during a tenure that also included the antics (and talents) of Amy Poehler and Tina Fey. After leaving the show, she didn't slow down. She is a frequent guest star on television shows, like the hit *30 Rock*, and has appeared in several movies, including *I Now Pronounce You Chuck & Larry* and *Spring Breakdown*, which she cowrote. In the spring of 2010 Rachel returned to live theater to star in A.J. Gurney's *Sylvia* at the George Street Playhouse in New Brunswick, New Jersey. And in August 2010 she took on a new role: mom to her son, Eli Benjamin.

ELIANE markoff

Many children follow in the footsteps of their parents or other adult role models, but the source of **Eliane Markoff**'s creativity is her late daughter, Rachel, who drew to pass the time during her many medical appointments at the Jimmy Fund Clinic in 1992. One of Rachel's drawings made a particular impression on Eliane: a picture of three flowers—one purple, one yellow, another red, all with green stems—and a shining yellow sun in the top right corner. Following Rachel's death in 1993, Eliane copied and then painted her daughter's striking work of art as best she could. That painting now hangs on the ninth floor of Children's Hospital Boston in Rachel's memory. Rachel's image is the logo for the Rachel Molly Markoff Foundation, which Eliane and her husband, Gary, founded to help families cope with childhood cancer. In 2008 Eliane joined the SOWA Artists Guild of Boston. She keeps a South End studio and also founded Art in Giving, which donates proceeds from sales of works of art by Eliane and others to the foundation. A talent for visual art seems to run in the family. Audrey, Rachel's twin sister, is an artist who works in mosaic and yarn designs.

CRAIGIE zildjian

When **Craigie Zildjian** joined her father, Armand, and paternal grandfather, Avedis III, in the family cymbal business in 1976, it was the first time that three generations of Zildjians had worked side by side. Twenty-two years later, Craigie became the first woman to be CEO of the Norwell-based company. She is credited with overseeing a period of unprecedented growth that has strengthened Zildjian's position as the market leader in cymbals. When the company marked its 375th anniversary, Craigie developed the American Drummers Achievement Awards to honor the great legends of the drummer's set, including such percussionists as Louie Bellson, Roy Haynes, Elvin Jones, and Max Roach. A trustee emerita of the Berklee School of Music, she added the Zildjian Family Opportunity Fund, administered through the Percussive Arts Society, to the long list of educational opportunities made available to students of music through the Zildjian organization.

BARBARA rockett

As the story goes, you wouldn't want to page "Dr. Rockett" at Newton-Wellesley Hospital. That's because you wouldn't know which Dr. Rockett might answer the call. There's the family matriarch, Dr. **Barbara A. P. Rockett**, a renowned general surgeon; her husband, Dr. Francis X. Rockett, a neurosurgeon; their son Dr. Sean Rockett, an orthopedic surgeon; and their son Dr. William Rockett, a general surgeon, all with Newton-Wellesley connections. A graduate of Wellesley College and Tufts University School of Medicine, Barbara trained as a general surgeon at Boston City Hospital and the Boston Veteran's Administration Hospital. She is a member of the board of trustees and board of overseers of Tufts University Medical School. In 1985 the members of the Massachusetts Medical Society elected her its first female president (she is also the only president elected to consecutive terms). In 2006 the Massachusetts Medical Society recognized this mother of five with the Lifetime Achievement Award, an honor earned both in the operating room and representing other physicians. As one of just five women in her class of 150 at Tufts, Barbara faced the usual challenges of being a working mother while witnessing and participating in the many changes in her workplace and untold historic advancements in medical care.

EMILY rooney

Award-winning television journalist **Emily Rooney** is Boston's go-to moderator of the hot debate topics of the day. As host of *Greater Boston*, WGBH-TV's 30-minute nightly newsmagazine show, Emily has interviewed hundreds of people since the show's launch in 1997. In 2010 she expanded into issues radio with her one-hour daily, *The Emily Rooney Show*, part of WGBH-FM's new lineup. And while it seems like Emily has always been on camera, she made her name in the newsrooms and control rooms of some of TV's best broadcasts. Emily worked at WCVB-TV in Boston from 1979 to 1993, as assistant news director and news director. During her tenure there, the station's news department was honored with numerous top broadcasting awards, including two Alfred I. duPont-Columbia University Awards, several George Foster Peabody Awards, and the Radio/Television News Directors Association's Edward R. Murrow Award for "Best News Operation in the Nation." Emily then headed to New York, where she was executive producer of ABC's *World News Tonight* with Peter Jennings, and then joined Fox Network, where she oversaw national political coverage, including the 1996 presidential primaries, national conventions, and presidential election before returning to Boston. A Connecticut native, American University alumna, and mother of a daughter with the late WCVB reporter Kirby Perkins, Emily is the daughter of *60 Minutes* commentator Andy Rooney.

ZORICA pantić | JANET eisner | KAY sloan
HELEN drinan | JACKIE jenkins-scott

Wentworth Institute of Technology President **Zorica Pantić** was captured chasing her cap during a photo shoot atop the Massachusetts College of Art and Design's Tower Building. The women, all presidents of Colleges of the Fenway, represent a power bloc of higher education in the same small neighborhood. Joining Zorica on the 11th-floor balcony and roof garden are, from left in the larger photo: Sister **Janet Eisner**, Emmanuel College; **Kay Sloan**, Massachusetts College of Art and Design; **Helen G. Drinan**, Simmons College; and **Jackie Jenkins-Scott**, Wheelock College. (A man, the sixth member of Colleges of the Fenway, Charles F. Monahan Jr., president of Massachusetts College of Pharmacy and Health Sciences, waited patiently nearby.) From this perch, the presidents can easily see the area these colleges cover, which runs from the Riverway to Harvard Medical School and from the hospitals in the Longwood Medical Area to the Museum of Fine Arts. To put this packed corner of higher education into perspective: the schools that make up Colleges of the Fenway cover 68.5 acres and have a total enrollment of 17,100 undergraduate and graduate students. A little about the women gathered for this portrait: A college educator and professor of electrical engineering, Zorica has been president of Wentworth since 2005. Born, raised, and educated in the former Yugoslavia,

she is the Institute's fourth president and the first woman to hold the position. A member of the Sisters of Notre Dame de Namur, Sister Janet has been president of Emmanuel since 1979. Previous positions at the college include faculty member, chair of the English department, and director of admissions. Kay is the 13th president and the first woman to lead the public arts college, founded in 1873. In her 15 years at the helm of MassArt, Kay oversaw a period of incredible growth for the college that included a $140 million capital campaign and the transformation of the face of MassArt along Huntington Avenue through the development of two new artists' residences to house 725 students. (Kay announced the 2011 academic year is her last; MassArt selected Dawn Barrett, dean of the Architecture and Design Division at Rhode Island School of Design, as Kay's replacement.) Helen is an alumna of two of Simmons' graduate programs and a former chair of the college's board of directors. Previously a Boston business executive of note, Helen has been president of Simmons since 2008. In 2004 Jackie became the 13th president of Wheelock, and she brought a history of success with her. From 1983 until 2004 Jackie was president and CEO of Dimock Community Health Center in Roxbury, one of Boston's largest community-based health centers.

CAROL fulp

Carol Fulp didn't need to give much thought to the location for her portrait. This Boston-bred senior vice president of Brand Communications and Corporate Social Responsibility for John Hancock Financial knew she wanted to be photographed on the Commonwealth Avenue Mall with Meredith Bergmann's statue of Phillis Wheatley, from whom Carol gets daily inspiration. Wheatley, a slave in Colonial Boston who was later emancipated, was the first published African-American poet. Carol credits Wheatley with "pushing the boundaries that helped to change Boston." In her role at John Hancock, Carol oversees advertising, sponsorships, event management, and philanthropy for a company that *The New York Times* has cited as one of the country's 100 most recognizable brands. She, too, is recognized beyond Boston. In late 2010 President Obama nominated her as a U.S. representative at the 65th session of the General Assembly of the United Nations. Carol is very active in the community, serving as a trustee of the Massachusetts Convention Center Authority, the Boston Public Library, and the John F. Kennedy Presidential Library Foundation. She also participates in Democratic Party efforts on the local, state, and national level, is a member of the Democratic National Finance Committee, and was appointed by Mayor Thomas M. Menino as the cochair of Boston 2004, the host organization for the Democratic National Convention that year. In 2010 she received the Women of Valor Award from the New England branch of the Anti-Defamation League.

CORINNE grousbeck

Corinne Grousbeck has turned a successful advertising and marketing career into a life of helping nonprofit organizations and charities reach their goals. After graduating from the University of Michigan, Corinne began her marketing career at Procter & Gamble and moved on to positions at the advertising agencies Ross Roy, Grey, and finally Saatchi & Saatchi, where she was a vice president. She has been a devoted board member to charities including Lovelane Special Needs Horseback Riding Program, Cradles to Crayons, Blind Babies Foundation, and the Children's Health Council. Corinne is vice-chair of the Trust Board at Children's Hospital Boston and is a trustee and founding chair of the Trust Board at Perkins School for the Blind, where she was photographed for this book. She created and cochairs the annual Perkins Gala, which has raised almost $8 million for the school in six years. Married to Boston Celtics managing partner Wyc Grousbeck, Corinne, who strategically leverages her position to benefit a variety of causes, has created the Celtics Women's Group. She said she is continually inspired by her daughter, who attends Stanford, and her son, who is a student at the Perkins School. In 2011 she was the recipient of the New England Women's Leadership Award for Community Service for her work with nonprofits.

DIANE patrick

Long before her husband, Deval, ran for governor of Massachusetts, **Diane Patrick** was known for her skills as a lawyer, her civic service, and as a mother of two daughters. But when Diane was catapulted into the public eye with her husband's 2006 election, she wasn't prepared for the pressures the job would place on her family or the public scrutiny that would follow. We now know how tough this transition was for Diane because she speaks openly, often to large groups, about her depression and her struggle to find some balance between her private life and these new public demands. By the time the 2010 reelection campaign came around, however, Diane and her family had found a way to accommodate the stresses of being the state's first family. Diane was photographed in her office at the law firm Ropes & Gray, where she is a partner advising universities, hospitals, and health care organizations on compliance with labor and employment laws. Diane has supported or served on the boards of The Posse Foundation, Epiphany School, Jane Doe, Inc., United Way of Massachusetts Bay and Merrimack Valley, Boston Symphony Orchestra, Brigham and Women's Hospital, Children's Hospital Boston, and Arts Boston, among other organizations.

JANE garvey

Jane Garvey knows where she's going but has never forgotten where she came from. She was a teacher in South Hadley, Massachusetts, at the high school and college level before switching paths to embark on a 30-year career in transportation. Now the North American chair of Meridiam Infrastructure and the chair of the board of directors of the Bipartisan Policy Center in Washington, D.C., Jane previously headed the U.S. Public/Private Partnerships advisory group at J. P. Morgan. She began her post-educational journey in Massachusetts, serving first as an associate commissioner in the Department of Public Works and then as commissioner. Jane later became the first woman to run Logan International Airport (where this photograph was taken). In 1997 the U.S. Senate approved her nomination as the 14th (and first female) commissioner of the Federal Aviation Administration. Her tenure in that post included two of the biggest events in recent aviation history: Jane flew across the country at the turn of the century to prove the safety of the aviation system despite "Y2K" concerns, and on September 11, 2001, she took the unprecedented action of ordering the grounding of the more than 5,000 planes that were in the air during the attacks. All were landed safely.

LORI mckenna

Lori McKenna first caught the eye (and ears) of local music observers in the late 1990s when she won a spot on the bill at Lilith Fair, but she had already been building an audience through appearances at open mike nights and coffeehouses and her self-released debut CD *Paper Wings and Halo*. This married mother of five from Stoughton, Massachusetts, would not stay hidden for long, however. She had released three more CDs, received awards from ASCAP and the Boston Music Awards, performed at the Newport Folk Festival and the Sundance Film Festival, and gathered the attention of the music community all before happenstance would give Lori her biggest break. Her friend, fellow Boston-area singer-songwriter Mary Gauthier, gave a copy of Lori's music to someone with Nashville connections, and that person managed to put Lori's music into the hands of superstar Faith Hill. Ultimately, Hill recorded four of Lori's songs. Lori joined Hill and her husband, Tim McGraw, on their 2007 national tour and performed with Hill on *The Oprah Winfrey Show*. In early 2011 Lori released her sixth album, *Lorraine*, which is her given first name and the name of her mother, who died when Lori was seven.

DORIS yaffe

A self-proclaimed contrarian, **Doris Yaffe** is a lifelong resident of Boston, a home base she treasures. But she's dishing out some tough love. "As much as I care about our city, I have to travel, get out of town," said Doris, who wore three hats while working at Saks Fifth Avenue—director of fashion, public relations, and special events, "but I always come back." Indeed, this stylish globe-trotter does. Doris, who proudly notes she was 82 when her portrait was taken, turned one of the city's best Rolodexes (remember those?) into an extended network that supports nonprofits and international human rights causes. (As 2011 got rolling, Doris was pushed by one of her two sons to get her first e-mail account.) An indefatigable advocate for the causes she embraces, Doris has marched for Civil Rights, protested against the Vietnam War, was an early AIDS activist, and, after the genocide in Rwanda, she helped spread awareness about the African country's reconciliation. Her life hasn't been without its difficulties (her beloved husband of many years, Wally, died in 2007), but Doris doesn't do self-pity. She says the most important work of her life is what she's doing now: working with young people as part of the United Nations Millennium Project. "They are making the changes that will create the future. I just love being around them."

PAULA johnson

As a specialist in women's health, Dr. **Paula A. Johnson** is a pioneer in the treatment and prevention of cardiovascular disease who developed one of the first facilities in the country to focus on heart disease in women. This trailblazer said she knew from childhood that she wanted to be a doctor. At Radcliffe College, she studied biology and upon her graduation she was admitted to Harvard Medical School. After taking a year off to study at the Harvard School of Public Health, Paula earned her medical degree and her master's in public health in 1985. While doing her residency at Brigham and Women's Hospital Paula became fascinated by cardiology and chose it as her specialty. She was appointed chief medical resident in 1990, the first woman to hold that position in the hospital's history. She also added a new title: teacher. She is the head of the Mary Horrigan Connors Center for Women's Health and Gender Biology and is chief of the division of women's health at Brigham and Women's. Additionally, she directs the Center for Cardiovascular Disease in Women where she continues her mission to educate women about how to live a disease-free life.

ELLEN lutch bender

If there is someone who can see all sides of Boston's health care industry, it's **Ellen Lutch Bender**. As president and CEO of Bender Strategies, Ellen is a consultant to health care providers. As a two-term chair of the Arthritis Foundation (the board's first woman and first non-physician), Ellen has advocated for patients with arthritis and their families. The Ellen Lutch Bender Arthritis Research Award gives doctors a three-year, $150,000 fellowship to fund innovative research dedicated to the prevention, control, and cure of rheumatoid arthritis. This award was created by the Arthritis Foundation and the Boston law firm of Brown Rudnick Berlack Israels, where Ellen, one of the few non-lawyer professionals at the firm, was instrumental in the establishment of Brown Rudnick's Health Care Practice Group in 1991. Before joining Brown Rudnick, she served as the director of regional support services at University Hospital in Boston, was associate executive director of the Massachusetts Federation of Nursing Homes, and director of community affairs at Massachusetts General Hospital. She has served on the Governor's Commission on the Status of Women.

HARRIET lewis

A former teacher who never lost her passion for or commitment to education, **Harriet Lewis**'s philanthropic focus has long been to support the world's next generation of leaders: today's youth. Harriet and her husband, Alan, own Grand Circle Corporation, a leader in international travel for Americans older than 50. Harriet was photographed outside the Grand Circle headquarters at 347 Congress Street, which also houses the Grand Circle Gallery, a vintage travel poster gallery the couple opened to the public in 2010 in celebration of their 25th anniversary of working in Fort Point Channel. Through Grand Circle Foundation, which Harriet launched with Alan in 1992, more than $50 million has been donated or pledged in support of educational, cultural, and humanitarian organizations worldwide, including 100 schools in 60 communities in 30 countries, and many more programs for youth in Boston. The couple encourages their employees to give back to the community whether in Boston, Bangkok, or Basel, and nearly all are involved in at least one of more than 40 community service events worldwide. Said Harriet, "We all want to be part of something bigger than ourselves."

ABIGAIL johnson

As **Abigail Johnson** takes on more of the leadership of Fidelity Investments, the Boston-based financial giant that her grandfather founded, she takes up another equally important Johnson–family tradition: giving back. Like her parents, Ned and Lillie Johnson, Abby is counted among the most philanthropic people in the region and country, often giving quietly or anonymously to support some of Boston's most important institutions and programs. The Johnsons (and the company's Fidelity Foundation) have supported Massachusetts General Hospital, Children's Hospital Boston, Beth Israel Deaconess Hospital, and the Museum of Fine Arts, to name a few. Abby didn't start at the top at Fidelity. A graduate of Buckingham Browne & Nichols School and William Smith College, she answered telephones in Fidelity's customer service department and later was a research associate with Booz, Allen and Hamilton. After receiving her MBA from Harvard Business School, she began her ascent at Fidelity.

GAY vernon | CANDY o'terry

Like so many great ideas, theirs started out simply. Magic 106.7's **Gay Vernon**, left, and **Candy O'Terry** wanted to tell the stories of extraordinary women. In 1993 the pair began their 30-minute Sunday morning radio show, *Exceptional Women*, and they're still at it. To date, the broadcasters have introduced Boston to more than 500 women from every walk of life in their weekly fugue. Candy and Gay have garnered 33 local and national awards for excellence in women's programming, but they say the greatest gift of all is meeting each woman, hearing her story, and passing it on. Candy, a singer all her life who started by warbling jingles in the 1980s, celebrated her 20th year at the station in 2010. Gay has been on-air at Magic 106.7 for nearly two decades and a radio newscaster for 30 years. Fittingly, their own stories are exceptional. Candy was working as the secretary to the program director when she was given a chance to do public affairs interviews. She approached Gay, who was Magic 106.7's news director, "and the best interviewer I knew," and asked Gay to be her radio partner. The rest is radio history.

ISAURA mendes

For a mother to lose a son to the violence of the city's streets is unthinkable, but when **Isaura Mendes** had two sons murdered, she didn't let the unspeakable acts silence her. This Cape Verdean native was reborn as a Dorchester peace activist. It was 1995 when Isaura's son Bobby was stabbed over what has been called a "stupid argument," and his death sparked a war among the city's Cape Verdean youth that left several dead in Dorchester and Roxbury. And in 2006 Isaura's youngest son, Alexander "Mathew" Mendes, was shot to death. Isaura and Shannon Flattery, of Touchable Stories, put together the antiviolence initiative The Bobby Mendes Peace Legacy in 1999. Its programs include public speaking in schools and prisons, grief counseling for families and friends who have lost loved ones, and the Annual Parents and Children's Walk for Peace. It was at one of the peace walks in his brother's memory that Mathew spoke up about the need to not retaliate when violence strikes at you: "When a young boy loses plenty of family and friends to street violence and he is able to avoid revenge, maintain his sanity, and continue to pray and keep the faith that there is a better life some day, some way, some place—that's me."

JEAN maccormack

Jean F. MacCormack was enjoying a successful career in higher education when she set her sights on what seemed to many to be an impossible goal: opening a public law school in the state. But this third chancellor of the University of Massachusetts Dartmouth succeeded and presided over the opening of the 2010 academic year with that public law school in place. It had more applicants than seats. Jean was installed at the Dartmouth campus of the state's public university system in 2001, having served as interim chancellor since late 1999. During her tenure, the student population has grown from 6,900 to 9,100 and is projected to top 10,000 by 2012. The campus has seen a doubling of student housing and research funding has grown from $7 million to more than $20 million. Jean earned a bachelor's degree in literature and fine arts from Emmanuel College and a master's and doctorate in education from the University of Massachusetts Amherst. She has more than 20 years of experience in educational administration at the secondary and higher education levels and joined UMass Dartmouth after serving as interim chancellor, deputy chancellor, and vice chancellor for administration and finance at the University of Massachusetts Boston.

MAUREEN hancock

She has been called "The Comedian Medium," but that moniker misses the very serious work **Maureen Hancock** does in helping people connect with loved ones who have died. Her style is to use humor to deliver messages and soften even the hardest skeptic. Author of *The Medium Next Door, Adventures of a Real-Life Ghost Whisperer*, this mother of two boys filmed a pilot in early 2011 with ABC Media Productions and Sander/Moses Productions (executive producers of the hit show *Ghost Whisperer*) for her upcoming reality project about her life. Maureen's path to becoming a medium began on an icy night in 1992 when she fell asleep at the wheel and hit a tree, breaking several facial bones and fracturing her skull. She believes that the extreme trauma caused her to begin to hear and see the deceased and that the accident also caused a reawakening from a prolonged illness as a child. Maureen's work has connected her with those facing illness and loss from the Boston area to Chernobyl. Through her own charitable foundations, Seeds of Hope and Mission for the Missing, Maureen provides these services pro bono. She also works with medical groups such as The S.A.N.E. Program, several hospice groups throughout New England, and Relay for Life for the American Cancer Society.

MARY richardson

After 30 years as one of Boston's most trusted and popular television journalists, mostly from the anchor desk and "back roads" of WCVB-TV's *Chronicle*, **Mary Richardson** thought she'd take a summer off. But her daydreams were quickly set aside as she stepped down from *Chronicle* and began a new career as the community liaison for Steward Health Care System (formerly the Caritas Christi Health Care System), where she is charged with making sure that those who use St. Elizabeth's Medical Center in Brighton, Norwood Hospital, Carney Hospital in Dorchester, and the three other hospitals in the system are aware of the programs and services that are available to them. An award-winning journalist, Mary was coanchor of the long-running *Chronicle*, beginning in 1984 with Peter Mehegan and later with Anthony Everett. She joined WCVB in 1980 as a news reporter and anchor and served as the host of the former weekly public affairs show *Five on Five*. For a decade she cohosted the annual Holiday at Pops! concert as well as the popular Pops Goes the Fourth! celebration at the Hatch Shell. Raised and educated in California, this mother of three lives in Belmont with her husband, Stan Leven, an award-winning producer for *Chronicle*.

KIMBERLY
steimle

As Suffolk Construction's executive vice president for marketing and work acquisition, **Kimberly Steimle** is responsible for growing the company's roster of work projects; she also oversees Suffolk's charitable programs and, among other philanthropic efforts, serves on the board of Habitat for Humanity and on the board of overseers for the Boys & Girls Clubs of Boston. Kim has coordinated the civic efforts of the causes most supported by Suffolk and its CEO, John Fish, which include the Inner-City Scholarship Fund, Presidents at Pops for the Boston Symphony Orchestra, the National Conference for Community and Justice, the Anti-Defamation League "Torch of Liberty" Awards Dinner, and the Initiative for a Competitive Inner City. An alumna of Milton Academy and College of the Holy Cross, Kim was director of operations at McDermott O'Neill Associates, a strategic communications firm specializing in public affairs marketing, before joining Suffolk. During her tenure at the construction company, which has built some of Boston's most notable projects, she has been recognized in the local business community for her leadership skills and achievements. In 2008 she received the prestigious Pinnacle Award, which is presented annually by the Greater Boston Chamber of Commerce, and she was recognized as one of *Banker & Tradesman*'s "New Leaders" that year.

TIZIANA dearing

With her résumé and training, **Tiziana C. Dearing** could be enjoying a successful career in corporate America, but this alumna of Harvard's John F. Kennedy School of Government uses her talents to assist not-for-profit agencies that help some of Boston's neediest and most disenfranchised people. Tiziana is the first CEO of Boston Rising, a new philanthropic enterprise dedicated solely to fighting poverty in Boston. Previously, Tiziana was the president of (and the first woman to lead) Catholic Charities, which serves nearly 200,000 people a year through some 140 programs and services in 40 locations across Massachusetts. She is credited with refocusing the agency's fund-raising efforts and putting this branch of the Boston archdiocese back on more solid financial footing. Tiziana is also a board member of the World Peace Foundation. A mother of two, she was the executive director of the Hauser Center for Nonprofit Organizations at Harvard University and has been recognized for her work, including garnering an Emerging Executive 2010 Pinnacle Award from the Greater Boston Chamber of Commerce.

OPHELIA dahl

In 2010 *Boston* magazine called **Ophelia Dahl** one of the city's best thinkers, but most people know this cofounder of Partners in Health as one of city's best doers. The daughter of the late children's book author Roald Dahl and the late Oscar-winning actress Patricia Neal, she originally wanted to study medicine. But life had other plans. As Ophelia was preparing to attend college, she was encouraged by her father to see another part of the world. She "traveled from the quiet English countryside to Haiti, a place so unfamiliar to me I had to look up its exact location in an encyclopedia," she told the 2006 graduating class at Wellesley College. (Ophelia graduated from Wellesley in 1994 as a Davis Scholar.) It was in Haiti, while living in an orphanage and working for an ophthalmic organization, that Ophelia met Paul Farmer, a physician. In 1987 they, along with three others, founded Partners in Health, a health care and antipoverty nonprofit headquartered in Boston. Now the executive director of Partners in Health, Ophelia oversees the group's health programs in Africa, South America, Eastern Europe, and Boston. Partners in Health has been recognized with a number of honors and awards, including the 2005 Conrad N. Hilton Humanitarian Prize, one of the largest annual awards of its kind. And when a devastating earthquake struck Haiti in early 2010, killing hundreds of thousands, it was Partners in Health that was at the ready and served as a conduit for relief efforts.

JOYCE kulhawik

If **Joyce Kulhawik** looks relaxed as she leans against a tree on the grounds of Tanglewood (the Boston Symphony Orchestra's summer home for some 75 years), it is because this first lady of Boston's arts scene has probably logged more hours at the beautiful Berkshire arts center than many of the musicians who play there. Believed to be the first full-time television news arts and entertainment reporter/critic in the country, Joyce sparked a landslide of such coverage in Boston. During her more than 30 years at WBZ-TV, the local CBS affiliate, Joyce has covered it all: from ballet to rock 'n' roll, the Oscars to Live Aid, Abbey Road to the pyramids, and Yo-Yo Ma to Madonna. Nationally, Joyce has matched thumbs with Roger Ebert and parried with Leonard Maltin. As a three-time cancer survivor, she has testified before Congress and helped raise millions to fight the disease. Today Joyce proudly continues her work as an arts advocate and crusader in the fight against cancer.

RHONDA kallman

Rhonda Kallman is not only a successful entrepreneur, she is also a passionate businesswoman with a deep commitment to helping others move up the corporate ladder. She is a quick study who, at age 24, carved out a path in a decidedly male-dominated field. As the founder and CEO of New Century Brewing Co., she has created new brews that have won industry accolades. Rhonda and Jim Koch, who first met while working together at the Boston Consulting Group, founded The Boston Beer Company, best known as the brewers of Sam Adams. The two proved to be an early hit with their potent combination of Jim's business experience (and his great-great-grandfather's recipe) and Rhonda's diligence and energy. As the company grew, Rhonda became founding partner and executive vice president of sales and brand development. After securing Boston Beer Co.'s strategy and execution plans for the coming years, she resigned in January 2000 to pursue her next challenge: founding New Century Brewing Co. in April 2001 and producing and marketing innovative American beer styles. This wife and mother of three young children is a highly–sought after consultant for her expertise in distribution, consumer products, sales and marketing strategy, leadership, and motivational speaking.

ELIZABETH nabel

That Dr. **Elizabeth G. Nabel** became the first female to helm Brigham and Women's Hospital is just one of the many notable achievements of this Harvard Medical School–trained physician. As president of the Brigham and Women's and Faulkner hospitals, she is also the first woman to run a Harvard Medical School affiliate. Betsy, as she is affectionately known, completed her internal medicine and cardiovascular training at Brigham and Women's and Harvard Medical School before going on to faculty positions at the University of Michigan's medical school. A partner on 17 patents and author of more than 250 scientific publications, she returned to Boston from Bethesda, Maryland, where she was the director of the National Heart, Lung and Blood Institute at the National Institutes of Health, overseeing an extensive national research portfolio with an annual budget of $3 billion. Betsy was instrumental in developing the national "Go Red for Women" campaign to increase women's heart health awareness. She was also among those chosen to carry the Olympic torch for the 2010 Winter Games in Vancouver.

GLORIA larson

Prominent lawyer, public policy expert, and business leader **Gloria Cordes Larson** has served as president of Bentley University since 2007. She has already made a lasting impact on that institution in that she took the Waltham, Massachusetts, college to university status. Her other initiatives include a dramatic innovation in management education with the Bentley MBA program and the founding of the Center for Women and Business. Gloria has had a profound positive influence on the Boston area since she arrived from Washington, D.C., where she was deputy director of consumer protection at the Federal Trade Commission. Recruited by Massachusetts Governor Bill Weld to serve as secretary for Consumer Affairs, Gloria was later promoted to secretary of Economic Affairs. She then served as cochair of the government strategies group at Foley Hoag LLP, a leading national law firm, before going to Bentley. Known for her bipartisan efforts in working on some of the most important civic organizations in the city of Boston, Gloria has served as the chair of the Massachusetts Convention Center Authority (where she oversaw the construction of Boston's new convention center on the waterfront), chair of the Greater Boston Chamber of Commerce, a member of the Rose Kennedy Greenway Conservancy Board, and cochair of the Massachusetts Conference for Women.

VICTORIA
reggie kennedy

To many in Massachusetts, **Victoria Reggie Kennedy** is best known as the stalwart supporter of her late husband Edward M. Kennedy, the guiding star that kept the senior senator on course over the last decades of a life dedicated to public service. But Vicki comes from her own Louisiana political dynasty. She is the second of six children born to Louisiana judge Edmund M. Reggie and Doris Ann Reggie, a Democratic national committeewoman, both longtime political supporters of the Kennedy family. (Her brother Denis is a well-regarded photographer whose images include the cover portrait of Senator Kennedy's 2009 posthumously published memoir *True Compass*.) Vicki is an alumna of Tulane University Law School, where she was a member of the *Tulane Law Review*. She clerked for a U.S. Court of Appeals for the Seventh Circuit judge in Chicago and specialized in bank law. During her first marriage, this mother of two moved to Washington, D.C., where she worked for the now defunct Keck, Mahin & Cate and was made a partner. Since Senator Kennedy's death in August 2009, Vicki has made numerous appearances on behalf of the family, including the 2011 groundbreaking for the Edward M. Kennedy Institute for the United States Senate, located on the Columbia Point campus of the University of Massachusetts Boston.

TRISH karter

Dancing Deer Baking Co. cofounder **Trish Karter** left Wheaton College to help her father (and hero) Peter, who pioneered the recycling of post-consumer bottles and cans on an industrial basis, work his way through a Chapter 11 reorganization. She then took on a series of business challenges and later completed her master's in business administration at Yale. But Trish soon set aside her business interests and pursued her first love, drawing and painting, before an unintended turn of events drew her back into business and the formation of Dancing Deer in 1994. Trish called her time at the helm of Dancing Deer "a good run where I was lucky to be able to combine my business, artistic, environmental, community, and competitive passions and build a team." She racked up numerous industry accolades before stepping down as CEO in July 2010. In 2009 Trish completed a 15-day, 1,500-mile bicycle ride from Atlanta to Boston, spending each night with families living in shelters. Helping the homeless is a cause she continues to support: Dancing Deer dedicates 35 percent of its Sweet Home Gifts line to fund scholarships for homeless and at-risk mothers.

MAURA tierney

Maura Tierney may have achieved international acclaim as a television, film, and stage actress, but back in the Hyde Park neighborhood where she was born and raised, she's the daughter of the late Joseph, who served on Boston's City Council for 15 years, and Pat, a well-known real estate broker. It's a role she seems to relish above all others. Like all great Hollywood tales, Maura's story began quietly. While attending Notre Dame Academy in Hingham she made an appearance in The Boston Globe Drama Festival. She attended New York University as a dance major but switched to drama and started landing roles as she was finishing her studies. Best known for her portrayal of Dr. Abby Lockhart on the long-running NBC drama *ER*, she was cast in a lead role in *Parenthood*, but dropped out of the show after being diagnosed with breast cancer and undergoing surgery in 2009. Maura has played memorable characters on several other TV series, including *NewsRadio*, *Rescue Me*, and *The Whole Truth*, which marked her return to TV after her breast cancer treatment. Among her more than two dozen film credits are *Semi-Pro*, *Baby Mama*, and *Liar, Liar*. In 2011 Maura returned to the stage, starring in *God of Carnage* at the Gate Theatre in Dublin, Ireland.

ANN hobson pilot

When **Ann Hobson Pilot** retired as the principal harpist for the Boston Symphony Orchestra at the close of the 2009 Tanglewood season, it was the end of an era. But Ann, the first African-American woman to play for the BSO and believed to be the first African-American woman to join any major orchestra, didn't stop performing, teaching, or preaching the wonders of this "angelic instrument," as she calls the harp. Ann was drawn to the harp as a girl and took to it quickly, earning a spot at the Cleveland Institute of Music. She joined the National Symphony Orchestra in Washington, D.C., (she was the first and only African-American musician) where, at the age of 25, Ann's playing caught the attention of legendary Boston Pops conductor Arthur Fiedler. She auditioned for and, of course, landed jobs with both the Boston Symphony Orchestra and the Boston Pops. Ann, who used her whole body to play the difficult instrument, as often noted by reviewers, is on the faculties of the New England Conservatory of Music, Boston University, Tanglewood Music Center, and the Boston University Tanglewood Institute. She has traveled the world, both as a performer and as a historian of her instrument. After her retirement, she returned to perform the world premiere of *On Willows and Birches*, written for her by John Williams. The documentary *A Harpist's Legacy, Ann Hobson Pilot and the Sound of Change*, about Ann's amazing life and career, debuted on WGBH in July 2011.

KATHRYN white | ANGELA menino | CATHERINE flynn

They have the honorifics and accolades bestowed on them, but these First Ladies of Boston—**Kathryn White**, left, **Angela Menino**, center, and **Catherine Flynn**—are known to most locals by their first names and for their quiet actions on behalf of the city. Kathryn, Angela, and Catherine are also known for their steadfast loyalties to their husbands, under whose administrations Boston has undergone the greatest transformation in its long history. In addition to being astute political and social advisers to the most recent leaders of Boston—Kevin White (1968 to 1984), Thomas M. Menino (1993 to present), and Ray Flynn (1984 to 1993)—they have carved out their own paths, working in the community and raising countless millions for charity. This photograph was taken on a bench in the Public Garden not far from the spot where Bill Brett took the now-iconic photograph of their husbands wearing raincoats and holding umbrellas, which graced the cover of his first book, *Boston, All One Family*.

MYRA kraft

A charity could have had no better friend than **Myra Hiatt Kraft**. She was not someone who just wrote checks for the causes she supported; she regularly opened her Brookline home to host sit-down dinners for several hundred in her backyard. And when this leading lady of philanthropy in New England died of cancer in July 2011, thousands mourned her passing. She and her husband, Robert Kraft, owner of the New England Patriots professional football team and New England Revolution professional soccer team, traveled with their four sons and their families on trips to Israel, where they funded several programs, including an American-style football field in Jerusalem. Myra was born in Worcester, the daughter of the late Jacob and Frances L. Hiatt, who from early on instilled in their daughter the idea of philanthropy. (A Worcester magnet school bears Jacob's name and Frances was involved with numerous organizations, including Girls Inc.) A graduate of Brandeis University, Myra was a longtime supporter of her alma mater and Combined Jewish Philanthropies. In addition to her work through the New England Patriots Charitable Foundation and the Robert K. and Myra H. Kraft Foundation, she served on the boards of several organizations including the Boys & Girls Clubs of Boston, the United Way of Massachusetts Bay, and the American Repertory Theater.

MARY reed

Because **Mary L. Reed** followed a path her mother, Bessie Tartt Wilson, carved out and continued her mother's work after Bessie's death in 1999, today scores of low-income families have reliable early care and education for their children. Bessie founded Tartt's Day Care Center, Boston's first minority-owned day care center, in Roxbury in 1946. And in 2002 Mary started a nonprofit, named in her mother's honor, which focuses on early care and education for low-income families. A recipient of the national Purpose Prize, Mary left a successful career in human services to build on her mother's legacy. She has been called to serve on numerous Boston boards, including the University of Massachusetts Foundation, the John F. Kennedy Library Foundation, Morgan Memorial Goodwill Industries, the Crittenton Women's Union, and the Bennett College Board of Trustees. A tireless fund-raiser and advocate, Mary leads the Bessie Tartt Wilson Initiative for Children with passion and quiet confidence, always keeping her eye on the goal that one day all children, across all income levels, will have quality early care and education.

PHYLLIS godwin

This wasn't the journey **Phyllis Godwin** had mapped out for herself. She is a graduate of Thayer Academy and Pembroke College (the women's school at Brown University) and she studied business at Radcliffe College when Harvard hadn't yet fully opened its programs to women. In 1973, after 22 years of being a stay-at-home wife and mother to two daughters, Phyllis took over her father's electrical supply business, which had one store in Quincy. She knew the business, of course, from her days playing with the machinery in the store opened by her father, Nicholas Papani, in 1923, but becoming the president and CEO of Granite City Electric Supply Co. wasn't in her plans. Nearly four decades later, she has grown Granite City into a regional company, with more than a dozen stores, that competes directly with the "big box" home improvement stores. (Granite City is an official partner of both the Red Sox and the New England Patriots.) In the process, Phyllis became a leader of, and a role model for, female executives. She is the first female president of the South Shore Chamber of Commerce. Her portrait, pictured behind her, was commissioned by her father.

CAROLYN mugar

Growing up in a family of food enthusiasts gave **Carolyn Mugar** no other option, she said, than supporting farming and providing good food for all. Carolyn's mother, Marian Graves, a Saugus native, was a home economics teacher and dietician who ran the cafeteria at Watertown High School. Her father, Stephen P. Mugar, was able to leave Eastern Turkey, or historic Armenia, as a child with his family shortly before the Armenian Genocide of 1915-1923. Stephen pioneered the development of supermarkets with Star Market. Carolyn credits this background with allowing her to understand the experiences of recent immigrants as well as those of people settled in New England for centuries. It was an environment in which she learned the love of place as well as an opportunity to cross cultural boundaries, she said. In 1994 Carolyn, with her late husband, John O'Connor, founded the Armenia Tree Project, a reforestation effort that has planted more than 3.5 million trees and provided hundreds of jobs in Armenia. For more than 25 years, she has been the executive director of Farm Aid, which is dedicated to keeping family farmers on the land. Carolyn travels extensively across the United States and relishes learning about what holds the coasts together. She added: "The most fascinating people to me are curious, creative, and absorbed in a project bigger than themselves."

ELIZA dushku

While her Watertown neighbors were worrying about what to wear to middle school, **Eliza Dushku** was appearing in her first movie, *That Night*, opposite Juliette Lewis. By the time Eliza was a teen, she had already accumulated a few film credits and appeared as Jamie Lee Curtis and Arnold Schwarzenegger's daughter in *True Lies*. She hasn't stopped working since: She now has two dozen movies and starring turns in hot television shows, including *Buffy the Vampire Slayer*, *Tru Calling*, *Angel*, and *Dollhouse*, under her belt. Eliza's work ethic extends to her offscreen charitable efforts, including raising money for Children's Hospital Boston. While in Boston in the spring of 2010, Eliza spent as much time fund-raising for cancer treatment, research, and care as she did cheering on the Boston Celtics. Eliza has embraced social media, amassing more than 50,000 fans on Facebook and some three-quarters of a million Twitter followers, who get regular updates on her work, politics, and Boston sports.

ELISHA daniels

In a way, **Elisha Daniels** didn't get cancer; breast cancer got her, and this survivor isn't letting go. In 2006, while enjoying a successful career in the fashion industry, she was diagnosed with breast cancer, and a mastectomy, chemotherapy, hormone therapy, and radiation was followed by a reconstruction. This experience turned Elisha into a dogged activist and fund-raiser, working primarily with The Breast Cancer Research Foundation, a nonprofit organization founded by her friend Evelyn Lauder to support medical research. Elisha helped to raise nearly $3 million and was asked to serve on The Breast Cancer Research Foundation's National Board of Advisors. She is committed to generating awareness and supporting other women who face this disease. In 2009 she and fellow breast cancer survivor Kelley Tuthill (see page 53) coauthored *You Can Do This! Surviving Breast Cancer Without Losing Your Sanity or Your Style*, with the foreword by Evelyn Lauder. Her second book, *Remaining a Lady...While Being a Dame, Lessons in Life and Fashion*, is due out in late 2011. All the while, she has continued to work in fashion; in 2009 she opened Elisha Daniels for Jean Pierre & Company, her own accessories boutique on Newbury Street.

SHARI redstone

You might think **Shari Ellin Redstone** has achieved all she has merely because of her last name, but you'd be wrong—very wrong. A lawyer by training, this daughter of media mogul Sumner Redstone easily adapted to running National Amusements, the organization her grandfather founded, which owns and operates Showcase Cinemas. In 2002, as president of National Amusements, she initiated her own project: the opening of a six-theater, 74-screen chain in Moscow and St. Petersburg, Russia, which now ranks among that nation's most successful theater organizations. In June 2011 the theaters in Russia were sold to the country's largest theater chain. Shari is non-executive vice chairman of CBS Corporation and Viacom, and in 2010 she founded a private-equity firm, Legacy Ventures, to provide capital and advice to media and technology start-ups. A graduate of Tufts University, Shari received her law degree at Boston University School of Law. Before taking an interest in her family's theater business, she was a social worker and a public defender. She has served on the boards of several charitable organizations, including the board of trustees of the Dana-Farber Cancer Institute, the board of directors at Combined Jewish Philanthropies, and the board of directors of the John F. Kennedy Library Foundation.

KERRY murphy healey

Just because **Kerry Murphy Healey** left public office does not mean she abandoned the causes she championed as the 70th lieutenant governor of Massachusetts. While serving in that office, Kerry led successful efforts to combat drunken driving, address homelessness, and increase penalties for perpetrators of child abuse, gang violence, sexual assault, and domestic violence. After losing to Democrat Deval Patrick in the 2006 governor's race, she was a Fellow at the Harvard Kennedy School's Institute of Politics and Center for Public Leadership, and in 2008 she served as a senior advisor for the Romney for President campaign. That year Kerry was also appointed to the executive committee of the U.S. Department of State's Public-Private Partnership for Justice Reform in Afghanistan. She serves on numerous nonprofit boards, including the Pioneer Institute, Milton Academy, the Commonwealth Shakespeare Company, and Caritas Cubana. Kerry received an AB in government from Harvard College and a doctorate in law and political science from Trinity College Dublin. She is the creator and host of *Shining City*, a television series showcasing New England's cutting-edge scientific and social innovation that aired on NESN in 2010. Kerry has been married to Sean for 25 years, and they have two teenaged children.

ERIN mcdonough

Erin McDonough could have glided through life using her last name (she is the daughter of late *Boston Globe* sports columnist Will McDonough) and her family's deep connections to this city to open doors, but instead she carved out her own niche working in health care. Born in South Boston, she moved with her family to Hingham when she was in the first grade. She is a "proud graduate" of Notre Dame Academy and a "very proud double Husky," having received her undergraduate degree and a master's in business administration from Northeastern University. Erin is the mother of a grown son, Gerry. She and her siblings—Terence, Ryan, Cara, and Sean—founded the Sean McDonough Charitable Foundation in 2002. In its first eight years, the foundation raised nearly $3 million that was distributed to 116 nonprofit groups and programs. The senior vice president of public affairs at Brigham and Women's Hospital, Erin previously was vice president of public affairs at New England Baptist Hospital. In 2011 she was honored by the Boys & Girls Clubs of Dorchester with a New England Leadership Award, which is given each spring to the city's most civically minded women.

BARBARA lee

Barbara Lee has her eye on a better future and has made it her mission to see that goal come to life. A former schoolteacher and social worker, this mother of two grown sons created and leads the Barbara Lee Family Foundation, which supports programs on women in politics and the contemporary arts. She has endowed the Barbara Lee Political Intern Fellowship Program at Simmons College (her alma mater) as part of her overall mission to promote full political participation for women. Her other major political endowment, the Barbara Lee Women in U.S. Politics Training Program and Lecture Series at Harvard's John F. Kennedy School of Government, trains women nationwide for serving in elected office. As a member of the Institute of Contemporary Art's board of trustees, Barbara's substantial leadership pledge launched the capital campaign to build the new ICA—the city's first new art museum in nearly a century. She is a founding chair of the contemporary arts program at the Isabella Stewart Gardner Museum and an avid supporter of public art, including the Boston Women's Memorial and the Arts on the Point sculpture garden at the University of Massachusetts Boston.

CHRISTINE
mcsherry

When **Christine McSherry**'s son Jett was diagnosed with Duchenne muscular dystrophy, or DMD, a fatal, progressive genetic disease that destroys muscle tissue and has no cure, she reacted like any parent and wondered what could be done. After this former registered nurse was told, "There's nothing you can do. There's no hope," she explained to *The Boston Globe* that she said to herself, "That's not true." So she and her husband, Stephen, founded the Jett Foundation to fund research on this disease that mostly affects boys and to seek out doctors who were aggressively treating the symptoms. Christine worked as a case manager for those with HIV at the former Tufts New England Medical Center and has said that she learned the power of helping people manage a disease by treating its symptoms. Since Christine started the Jett Foundation in 2001, shortly after her five-year-old son was diagnosed, the nonprofit has raised nearly $2 million dollars for Duchenne research. The foundation funds the Jett Program for Pediatric Neuromuscular Disorders at MassGeneral Hospital for Children. Although there is still no cure for DMD, the goal of the program is to keep this generation of children, those like Jett, who is now a teenager, healthy enough to see the day that a cure is discovered. The foundation also started the Jett Ride, an annual extended bicycle trek for young people, often siblings of those with DMD.

JOAN parker

Joan Parker speaks for those who wouldn't otherwise have a voice. The primary focus of her energy is her work with Community Servings, an organization that delivers free hot meals to people with life-threatening illnesses. She chaired two successful capital campaigns for the Jamaica Plain–based nonprofit that resulted in the construction of a new headquarters building (now named after her). Joan began her professional life as a service representative for New England Telephone and Telegraph following her graduation from Colby College where she majored in psychology. It was at Colby that she met her husband, Robert B. Parker, the master of New England crime fiction, who died in 2010 (that's his dog Pearl behind her). While raising their two sons, Joan earned a graduate degree in psychology from Tufts, taught child psychology at Endicott College, and became the director of curriculum and instruction for the Northeast Region of the Commonwealth of Massachusetts. Following her retirement, she collaborated with her husband on two books and 12 screenplays. Joan also serves on the board of New Repertory Theater and the advisory board of PFLAG (Parents, Families and Friends of Lesbian and Gays), which has as its mission the elimination of bullying in the state's public schools. In late 2010 she entered a training program at the Center for Dispute Resolution and Mediation to pursue her interest in becoming a mediator.

LINDA holliday

When **Linda Holliday** left her familiar Southern roots and a high-end Jupiter, Florida, retail business for Boston, she had few local contacts in her new world. A short time thereafter, due to her business acumen, a clear vision, some media training, and her own television broadcasts, Linda became a fixture at the intersection of the New England fashion and sports scenes in her segments on the weekly television show *styleboston*. And she did it in Boston, where it often takes decades to break through traditional networks. She succeeded in a field where this old city's passions run deep: sports. When not wading through pitches and proposals from Portland to Providence, Linda can be seen at charitable events, like riding in the 50-mile Best Buddies race to Hyannis Port with her boyfriend, New England Patriots head coach Bill Belichick, and supporting Cradles to Crayons. Linda also is a regular on the sidelines of the lacrosse games of her twin daughters, Ashley and Katie.

UMA thurman

Uma Thurman's work on stage and on film has taken her around the world, yet her philanthropy regularly brings her back to Boston, where she was born. Uma is a member of the board of directors of Room to Grow, which supports impoverished babies for their first three years. A mother of two, Uma says that it was while she was pregnant with her first child that her New York neighbor, Room to Grow founder Julie Burns, exposed her to the needs of children born into poverty. That affiliation has continued as Room to Grow opened its second branch, this one in Boston. In 2011 the nonprofit's Boston branch reported it was accepting about 12 newborns a month. Best known for starring in *Pulp Fiction*, *Hysterical Blindness*, and the *Kill Bill* movies, Uma left Boston at an early age and was raised in the western part of the state, where her father, Robert Thurman, one of the nation's leading scholars on Buddhism, was a professor at Amherst College. Uma also serves on the board of Tibet House with her mother, Nena.

SHELLEY hoon keith

Shelley I. Hoon Keith turned a volunteer position at the Roxbury Multi Service Center into a successful career in housing and development. In time, Shelley and her husband, John W. Keith, have become two of the city's most generous philanthropists, giving their money and time to numerous causes. Holding a graduate degree from the University of Nebraska-Lincoln and an undergraduate degree from State University of New York at Stony Brook, this Jamaican-born executive has had successful careers in the public, private, and not-for-profit sectors. Shelley's motivation to incorporate a construction company, Hoon Companies Inc., was fueled by the need to prove that women can successfully compete in this male-dominated industry. She divides her time between running an ongoing real estate/subcontracting business and actively working with St. Mary's Women's and Children's Center in Dorchester, Boston Medical Center's Leadership Council, and The Tryall Fund in Jamaica. Other organizations she has supported include Cambridge College, the Anti-Defamation League's New England Chapter, the Forsyth Institute, Oxfam America, the Boston Center for the Arts, and the Harvard AIDS Initiative. She and her husband have received numerous accolades, including the 2010 Distinguished Achievement Award from B'nai B'rith Housing New England.

SHEILA brass | MARILYNN brass

Sheila Brass, left, and her sister **Marilynn Brass**, self-described "roundish bespectacled women in our sixties who have a combined total of 114 years of home baking and cooking experience," take their mission of collecting and preserving heirloom recipes *very* seriously. The duo, neither of whom married, say they have always felt comfortable in the kitchen because they learned to bake and cook at a very early age. Their mother, Dorothy, was an accomplished home cook, and the meals she served when the family lived on Winthrop's Sea Foam Avenue more than six decades ago are still fresh in her daughters' memories. From the Cambridge kitchen that serves as the repository of the collected recipes, the sisters produced definitive volumes of America's cooking history: *Heirloom Baking With the Brass Sisters, More Than 100 Years of Recipes Discovered from Family Cookbooks, Original Journals, Scraps of Paper, and Grandmother's Kitchen* and *Heirloom Cooking With the Brass Sisters, Recipes You Remember and Love*, written with Andy Ryan. They also starred in the PBS show *The Brass Sisters: Queens of Comfort Food*. The sisters have collected recipes at yard sales, a town dump in Maine, and from family and friends.

SHONDA schilling

When **Shonda Schilling** arrived in Boston, this wife of former Red Sox pitcher Curt Schilling rewrote the book on how the spouse of a pro athlete could win over a new city and engage fans in supporting charitable efforts. Shonda, a mother of four, is active in myriad charities, with some of those connections coming as the result of facing a personal challenge. A skin cancer survivor, Shonda founded the Shade Foundation of America in 2002 with the goal of changing society's attitude toward sun exposure. Not only has she heightened awareness of skin cancer prevention, she has raised much-needed money for research and education programs. The Schillings have also been active in raising money to fund ALS research since Curt's days playing in Philadelphia. Shonda is the author of the *New York Times* best seller *The Best Kind of Different*, which "shares the painful and joyous story of her son Grant's struggle with Asperger's Syndrome," and how it changed their lives. The book, now out in paperback, covers something that Shonda addresses in her many public-speaking engagements each year: what other parents can learn about this increasingly common diagnosis. When her children's school and activities calendars permit, Shonda travels and makes appearances in support of her book.

PATRICIA foley

Patricia A. Foley is as comfortable on the water as she is on land. As the president of Save the Harbor/Save the Bay, the region's largest public interest harbor advocacy organization with more than 4,000 members, a staff of six, and a budget of nearly $1 million, Patty has helped ensure that one of Boston's most precious resources—the waterfront—is protected. It's an area she knows well. Born in South Boston, she graduated from Milton High School and later received a degree in sociology from University of Massachusetts Boston. Patty began her career in public service as a juvenile probation officer in the Quincy District Court, where she helped pioneer alternative sentencing programs for youthful offenders. In 1979 she joined Boston Mayor Kevin White's reelection campaign and a year later worked on U.S. Senator Edward M. Kennedy's presidential campaign. She was a legislative assistant to State Senator George Bachrach before joining then-Lieutenant Governor John Kerry's staff. Following his election to the U.S. Senate, Patty served as deputy chief of staff in Kerry's Washington office, then returned home to serve as his chief of staff in Massachusetts. In 1990 she served as Kerry's campaign manager for his first reelection effort, making her the first woman to successfully run a statewide campaign in Massachusetts.

SHARON reilly

While most people go to the Back Bay for its high-end retail shops and luxury spas and salons, **Sharon Reilly** and The Women's Lunch Place make sure that some 150 women and their children are fed six days a week at the day shelter on Newbury Street. Since taking over the reins of The Women's Lunch Place in July 2007, Sharon has expanded the programs offered and worked to implement a new strategic plan. A native Mississippian, she grew up on a sharecropper's farm during the 1950s and 1960s, which she credits with giving her a unique understanding of the plight of poor women and the devastating effects of poverty. Previously, Sharon was the director of community relations at The Food Project, and she still acts on its board of directors. Sharon is a former regional director of the Minnesota-based National Marrow Donor, where she concentrated on recruitment and retention of donors of color. With degrees from Rust College and the University of Mississippi, she is also a graduate of the Commonwealth Seminar and Boston College's executive leadership program, Leadership for Change, and is a member of The Commonwealth Institute Executive Director's Forum and the College Club of Boston.

HELEN rees

When **Helen Rees** started her literary agency in 1983, there were few agents of any note outside New York City, the hub of the publishing world. "This was before the Internet, e-mail, cell phones, or even fax machines," Helen said. "People told me I had to be in New York—*full time*." Instead she stayed put and is credited with opening the first national book agency in Boston. The noteworthy roster of clients that Helen, a supporter of the local arts scene (particularly opera), has amassed includes Harvard law professor Alan Dershowitz, U.S. Senator John Kerry, women's health expert Dr. Christiane Northrup, U.S. Senator and presidential nominee Barry Goldwater, and Jack and Suzy Welch. Helen made headlines when she secured a $4 million advance for the Welches' book, *Winning*. When she started her agency, Helen was in her 40s, divorced, and the mother of four boys. She had no publishing experience, just a suggestion from a friend that she might be good at shepherding projects into print. In addition to her unerring sense of what makes a great read, Helen, now a grandmother to three girls, has a dogged determination. "The difference between Helen Rees and a Rottweiler," Dershowitz told *The Boston Globe*, "is that eventually a Rottweiler will let go."

MARY milano

Without fail, **Mary Milano** could be found day after day and year after year overseeing the comings and goings of tens of thousands of tourists and diners at the Milano family–owned Union Oyster House, Boston's oldest restaurant. Mary, who died at age 93 in December 2009, was always impeccably dressed in one of her trademark suits, and she supervised affairs from her desk overlooking the red-brick line of The Freedom Trail. It was from this perch that she greeted a few presidents and a future president (then-U.S. Senator Barack Obama was feted at the historic eatery during the 2004 Democratic National Convention), visiting foreign dignitaries and royalty, leading athletes, and some of the biggest actors and musicians in the world. Leonardo DiCaprio was among the stars with whom Mary immediately shared a close relationship. When he was in town filming Martin Scorsese's Oscar-winning movie *The Departed*, the actor said to Mary's son Joe, "She reminds me of my grandmother."

HELEN chin schlichte

Helen Chin Schlichte has dedicated her life to helping Massachusetts residents. She first entered public service in 1949 as Assistant Secretary for Administration and Finance. She served 13 A&F secretaries and 12 governors during her tenure. After 54 years, she retired from her post in 2003, but she continues to assist in her community. The oldest of nine children, Helen and her siblings were raised in Charlestown during the Great Depression and World War II by parents who had emigrated from China. Helen is among the most civic-minded people in the region. She has served as chair of the board of directors of Kwong Kow Chinese School, the oldest Chinese school in Boston, and is a cofounder of the South Cove Manor Nursing Home. She has served on the boards of numerous organizations, including United Way of Massachusetts Bay and Merrimack Valley, Beth Israel Deaconess Medical Center, Boston Minuteman Council, Boy Scouts of America, Boys & Girls Clubs of Boston, the Bostonian Society, and the Boston Conference for Community and Justice.

JOANN burton

JoAnn Burton took her husband's legacy and ran with it—helping scores of young people along the way. With her husband, the late New England Patriots star Ron Burton Sr., JoAnn and their five children founded the Ron Burton Training Village, a 305-acre camp in Hubbardston, Massachusetts, which runs programs and camps for young people ages 11 to 18. JoAnn is shown in the main building of the village, which has served more than 3,000 young men and women in 26 years. The camp takes on the work ethic of its namesake, who died in 2003 from cancer. A native of Evanston, Illinois, JoAnn met Ron when he was a freshman at Northwestern University. (The twist in their tale is that she was a sociology major at rival University of Illinois.) JoAnn said she fell for Ron (who was known as a hard worker on and off the field), not for what he did, but for what he didn't do: "I saw him in the corner, and there were people drinking," JoAnn said, "and he ordered a glass of milk." JoAnn and the All-American running back came to Boston when Ron was chosen as the Patriots' first draft pick. This grandmother continues the work of her late husband. And it has paid off; three different colleges provide five full scholarships to graduates of the Ron Burton Training Village.

LINDA demarco

When **Linda DeMarco**, president of the board of directors of Boston Pride, speaks about Boston's annual Pride Parade, she not only addresses what the annual, 10-day celebration has become, but she also makes note, with a certain deference, of those who started it all more than 40 years ago. "In the early years, the Pride Parade was just a couple of cars; it took real courage to march then," said Linda about the gathering that celebrates Boston's lesbian, gay, bisexual, and transgendered communities. Today the parade has grown to include more than 200 organizations with an estimated quarter of a million spectators lining the route. Like so many others involved with the nonprofit Boston Pride, Linda first joined as a volunteer. When she's not corralling the groups for the parade or working on the logistics for Boston Pride events, Linda runs her own company, Boston Pretzel Bakery, Inc., and serves on the board of directors of the Faneuil Hall Merchants Association and the Small Merchants Association of Downtown Crossing. Linda spends her free time with her partner, Anna Dubrowski, whom she met at a Pride meeting. "We get to celebrate those who came before us," Linda said.

SWANEE hunt

Swanee Hunt's biography is called *Half-Life of a Zealot*, but it has been said that Swanee has lived several incarnations. A daughter of legendary Texas oil mogul H. L. Hunt, Swanee is president of Hunt Alternatives Fund. She and her sister Helen have been ranked in ninth place on Barron's list of the "World's Top 25" most important philanthropists. With two master's degrees and a doctorate in theology, she is the founding director of the Women and Public Policy Program at the Kennedy School of Government at Harvard University, chair of the Initiative for Inclusive Security (including the Women Waging Peace network), a member of the U.S. Council on Foreign Relations, and on the boards of Crisis Group and USA for UNHCR, the United Nation's refugee agency. Since 2009 Swanee and former Massachusetts Lieutenant Governor Kerry Murphy Healey (see page 126) have cochaired the Parity Project, a bipartisan effort to increase women's representation in high-level state and federal offices. Swanee served as U.S. ambassador to Austria from 1993 to 1997. Among her numerous publications is the well-received book *This Was Not Our War, Bosnian Women Reclaiming the Peace*. Wife of the late Maestro Charles Ansbacher, founder of the Boston Landmarks Orchestra, Swanee maintains a residence and offices in Cambridge, where she was photographed.

CAROLYN
pickman

Carolyn Pickman was born and bred in the city's old West End. She developed an appreciation for the craft of acting and theater while working with the Theatre Company of Boston and was a founding member of The Theatre's School Touring Company, a biracial performing group that brought arts to Boston's public high school students during the turbulent desegregation years. She also found a niche in the film and television industry as a casting director. For more than two decades she has cast thousands of actors, performers, and regular people in many of the most successful feature films, television, and commercial projects shot in New England. She has been recognized for Outstanding Achievement in Local Casting for her work on movies such as *Mystic River*, *Gone Baby Gone*, *Mystic Pizza*, *Shutter Island*, *The Departed*, and *The Town*. As an acting teacher at several colleges and a casting professional, Carolyn has guided aspiring actors and helped them to reach their potential. She is proud to have played a part in helping so many future actors achieve their dreams.

JOSEFINA bonilla

Josefina Bonilla tells the stories that others often overlook. As managing director of Color Media Group and publisher of its flagship publication, *Color Magazine*, she is responsible for creating business partnerships and developing opportunities to promote diverse professionals in New England and New York City. Previously, Fina was the editor-in-chief of *Entre Amigos Magazine*, a publication highlighting professional Hispanics in and around Boston. She also has worked as public relations director for Wentworth Institute of Technology and contributed on the editorial committee of *El Planeta* newspaper. She is on the board of The Partnership, Inc., and an active member of the Association of Latino Professionals in Accounting and Finance, National Association of Asian American Professionals, and the Greater Boston Chamber of Commerce. Fina has cowritten five screenplays with her sister Blanca, including *I Love You So Much* and *Ontrial*, which were finalists at the Sundance Screenwriter's competition. Born in Puerto Rico, she was raised in Massachusetts and is the mother of two sons, Edwin and Xavier.

KAY bernon

Kay Bernon believes in the curative power of music. In fact, this mother and grandmother believes that music can make miracles happen. Kay has committed herself and her family to winning support for, and bringing into being, a unique school that uses music studies to help young adults with cognitive and learning disabilities develop their talents and reach greater independence. When the Berkshire Hills Music Academy opened in South Hadley, Massachusetts, in September 2001, it offered new hope, Kay said, because the curriculum not only addresses the special needs of young people with disabilities but also supports their aspirations. For Kay, this is a public success that started as a private mission when she saw how music helped her son, who has Williams Syndrome. A Babson College alumna, Kay applied her business acumen to the school's creation, serving as founder, president of the board of trustees, and fund-raising chair. She tapped some big names from the music world to help raise money to open the school and to share the stage with young musicians with disabilities. While Kay has focused primarily on the Academy, she and her husband, Peter, also founded the Bernon Center for Public Service at Babson College, where she serves on the board of overseers, and she is a trustee at Bay Path College.

HOLLY safford

Had anyone told **Holly Safford** the difficulties she would face when she started her catering company, The Catered Affair, in 1979 out of the kitchen of her Scituate home, Holly might not have embarked on her journey to become one of the region's leading businesswomen. Holly built The Catered Affair as a way to feed her then young sons, and, once grown, she gave them careers. Holly and her sons, Andrew and Alex Marconi, now run the company out of its Rockland headquarters, which employs more than 300 catering and event specialists handling scores of events for as few as 50 and as many as 5,000. As founder and president of this multimillion–dollar annual enterprise, Holly makes it seem like she always dreamed of owning her own restaurant or catering company. But the reality is that the career chose her when her husband left the family. "I really thought my life was over—I was all of 30 years old. I did not finish college, I had not worked outside the home, and I thought, what can I possibly do?" Holly told *The Patriot Ledger*. Quite a lot, evidently. The U.S. Small Business Administration's 2003 Person of the Year, Holly supports numerous charities and continues to look for new ventures, including running The Courtyard restaurant in the Boston Public Library's McKim Building.

MIMI la camera | MARGARET drain

To the casual observer, **Mimi La Camera**, left, and **Margaret Drain** may seem more like twins than sisters separated by 16 months (Mimi is the senior). But their lives are definitely joined. Mimi is president of The Freedom Trail Foundation, the organization behind the iconic red-brick trail that is traversed by more than three-million visitors each year. Mimi also administers and raises all the private funding for the annual holiday lighting of the trees that run the length of the Commonwealth Avenue Mall from the Public Garden to Kenmore Square. Margaret is vice president of National Programs for Boston's WGBH-TV (the largest provider of national programs for the Public Broadcasting System), responsible for such hallmark series as *American Experience*, *Frontline*, *Masterpiece*, and *NOVA*. An alumna of Columbia University's School of Journalism, Margaret earned her television stripes in New York City at CBS and the Ford Foundation, where she was a documentary producer who worked with broadcasting legends like Bill Moyers and Fred Friendly. The daughters of musicians and natives of Cincinnati with roots in Kentucky tobacco farming, they both made their way to Boston: Mimi in 1966 and Margaret in 1987.

DUSTY rhodes

When **Dusty Rhodes** started her special events firm Conventures in 1977, it wasn't that there weren't women in business who she could emulate; it was that there wasn't another business in Boston using special events as a marketing and public relations tool. Dusty had been an industry trailblazer before. She was among the first women to work as an executive in professional sports, with stints in the front offices of the World Football League's Charlotte Hornets and New York Stars. While she was attending Penn State, her mentor, the university's head football coach Joe Paterno, instilled what became her management style and core philosophy: teamwork makes a difference. When not wearing a headset and corralling some the region's biggest business leaders and politicians at one of her events, this mother of six (three sons and three daughters) is corralling her family. She can often be found cheering as her children compete year-round in sports or getting out her tools and taking on a domestic project, as she did when she installed a new kitchen in her basement.

STACEY lucchino

As a tireless fund-raiser for cancer care and research and chair of the board of the YMCA of Greater Boston, **Stacey J. Lucchino** works on behalf of thousands who might never know her name. But that doesn't bother this busy mom, who also leads "Team 9" for the Pan-Mass Challenge, which has raised more than $330 million in 33 years for cancer research and treatment at Dana-Farber Cancer Institute through an annual bike-a-thon that crosses the state. Stacey is the wife of Red Sox President and CEO Larry Lucchino, who is also a supporter of numerous charities, particularly those supporting cancer research. Team 9, which Stacey has led since 2002, takes its name from the number worn by Red Sox Hall of Famer Ted Williams, who was one of the leading supporters of the Jimmy Fund programs at the Dana-Farber. (That's why she's sporting a "9" baseball cap.) In addition to the variety of charitable efforts supported by the Red Sox, Stacey is actively involved with a number of nonprofits, including Harvard University's Program in Education, Afterschool & Resiliency, Boston Medical Center, Rosie's Place, Dorchester's Epiphany School, and The United Way of Massachusetts Bay and Merrimack Valley.

ANNE bonnyman

The Reverend **Anne B. Bonnyman** is a trailblazer: She is the first woman to hold the storied job of rector of the 278-year-old Trinity Church in Copley Square. As the famed church's 19th rector, Anne leads a congregation of more than 2,000 members and supporters and has made sure that Trinity Church is known for far more than its National Historic Landmark building, which was designed by H. H. Richardson. During her tenure, the church has deepened its involvement with the city, including fostering a close ministerial partnership with Roxbury Presbyterian Church; providing parishioner and clergy support for the Dearborn School in Roxbury as it becomes a state-of-the-art science and technology secondary school; and participating in the opening of Yearwood House, a Trinity-supported transitional home in Boston for more than a dozen formerly homeless people. A native of Knoxville, Tennessee, and the mother of three adult sons, Anne was ordained in the Episcopal Diocese of Tennessee in 1982 and served in churches in Delaware and Tennessee before coming to Trinity Church in October 2006. She has announced she plans to retire from her position in September 2011.

JOANNE jaxtimer

As managing director of corporate affairs for BNY Mellon/New England, **Joanne Y. Jaxtimer** directs the financial institution's programs for governmental affairs, legislative and community affairs, philanthropy, and corporate social responsibility. One of the city's most civically active leaders, Joannie, as she's called, is past chair of the board of directors of the Boston Municipal Research Bureau and also serves on the boards of A Better City, the Greater Boston Chamber of Commerce, John F. Kennedy Library Foundation, the New England Council, Massachusetts Institute for a New Commonwealth, National Braille Press, and Special Olympics Massachusetts. In addition, she serves on the board of governors at the Boston College Club and Tufts Medical Center and on the Jimmy Fund visiting committee. She is active in a variety of community organizations, including Best Buddies; the Greater Boston Food Bank; the Center for Collaborative Leadership; and the YWCA, which selected her to join the Academy of Women Achievers, Class of 2001. She has received numerous awards, one being the Greater Boston Chamber of Commerce's Pinnacle Award. But the title she is most proud of is "Mom," when it's said by her teenaged son, Michael, who has pervasive developmental disorder, a form of autism. Joannie and her husband, Michael Barry, adopted their son from Ecuador, and they speak openly about his learning differences in an effort to help educate others.

DIANE paulus

Noted theater and opera director **Diane Paulus** returned to Boston in 2008 as the artistic director of the American Repertory Theater at Harvard University bringing with her an inspired energy that resulted in critical acclaim and regularly packed houses. Diane followed in the footsteps of two of her teachers: A.R.T. founder Robert Brustein, with whom she studied during her undergraduate years at Harvard, and his only other successor, Robert Woodruff, her mentor at Columbia University. Diane arrived at the A.R.T. fresh off directing the Tony Award–winning revival of *Hair* on Broadway. For her inaugural season, Diane turned the Zero Arrow Theatre into Club Oberon, a curated performance space; nearly doubled the annual box office tally; and directed the world premiere of *Johnny Baseball*, a musical about the Red Sox. Her sophomore year was equally impressive with back-to-back sold-out shows and the U.S. premiere of *Death and the Powers: The Robots' Opera*. In the summer of 2011 Diane was in rehearsals with four-time Tony Award winner Audra McDonald for *The Gershwins' Porgy and Bess*, a retelling of the American classic to open the 2011-2012 A.R.T. season.

MONICA jorge

Monica Jorge is an inspiration for all. An Ayer resident, Monica was pregnant with her second child in August 2007 when a seemingly routine C-section would forever change her life. She contracted necrotizing fasciitis, a flesh-eating bacteria, and was airlifted to Massachusetts General Hospital to undergo surgery to stabilize the infection, which included the removal of several organs and affected flesh. A short time later, doctors determined the infection had spread and that all four of Monica's limbs would have to be amputated for her to have a chance of survival. Monica endured 35 separate surgeries before being transferred to Spaulding Rehabilitation Hospital to begin the arduous process of getting her daily life back and some of the skills she needed to care for her children. Monica's ordeal was first recounted in *The Boston Globe Magazine* and later caught the attention of *The Oprah Winfrey Show*. While on a show called "Warrior Moms," Monica accomplished something few people did in the 25 years of the show—she rendered Oprah speechless with her story. Monica's is ultimately a tale of triumph; she worked with the team at Spaulding (many working extra hours, off the clock) to learn to use her new prosthetics to change diapers and other functions needed to lead an independent life. An expected six months of rehab became weeks, and on Christmas Eve, just four months from the day she almost lost her life, Monica left the hospital to spend the holiday at home with her two daughters and her husband, Tony.

JACKIE macmullan

When she was at Westwood High School, studying and playing basketball, **Jackie MacMullan** wondered why the girls' teams were being ignored by the local newspaper. She took up the matter with the sports editor, and he gave her a byline to ensure coverage. The game was on. Later, at the University of New Hampshire, Jackie played basketball, ran the sports section of the student newspaper, and worked as a summer intern at *The Boston Globe*, which sensibly hired her as a full-time sports writer after graduation. Her work impressed the editors at *Sports Illustrated*, who lured her to their ranks to write on basketball. After five years, she left the *SI* beat to be at home with her husband, Mike, and their children, Aly and Doug. Jackie returned to *The Globe* in 2002 as its first full-time female sports columnist. It was perfect timing: Three Super Bowl titles for the Patriots, two World Series wins for the Red Sox, and an NBA championship for the Celtics followed. In 2008 she again left the newspaper to write *When the Game Was Ours*, a best-selling book on the relationship between Larry Bird and Magic Johnson. Jackie now writes for ESPNBoston.com and is a commentator on all things sports for ESPN and Comcast SportsNet. She is working on a book collaboration with retired NBA superstar Shaquille O'Neal.

NANCY gaines

Nancy Gaines didn't bump up against the glass ceiling of Boston's major media outlets, she busted right through it. A pioneer and innovator in Boston journalism for nearly 40 years, Nancy made an impact early. As a cub correspondent for *The Boston Globe* in 1973, she was the first reporter on the scene for the Delta plane crash at Logan that killed 78, and she stayed on the story for 12 hours straight. During school desegregation, she brought a singular perspective as the only reporter on the beat whose children were being bused. In the 1980s Gaines created the *Boston Business Journal* and was the first woman to be editor of a major business publication or section in Boston. And in the 1990s she edited two of the magazines that tracked the city's exploding nightlife scene: *The Improper Bostonian* and *Stuff@night*. During the length and diversity of her run, Gaines has managed two newspaper groups and been editor of five magazines, and she has launched more careers than she can recall. Her hard work was not without sacrifices. "It was truly tough on my kids," she said, and it meant a lot of time away from home.

JEN mergel

The Beal Family Senior Curator of Contemporary Art at the Museum of Fine Arts, **Jen Mergel** is a museum curator who knows just as much about the city that surrounds her institution as she does about the objects inside. Jen was raised in Dorchester—her parents still live in the Jones Hill house where she was raised. Born at Boston Lying In, Jen attended St. Margaret's parochial school (now Blessed Mother Teresa) until the 8th grade when she attended Fontbonne Academy. She earned her undergraduate degree from Harvard University, where she made the Fogg Museum a regular stop, and received her master's degree from Bard College. Jen came to the MFA in early 2010 from the Institute of Contemporary Art on the South Boston waterfront, where she was an associate curator. As a contemporary art curator, she deals with objects like the piece behind her in this photograph. Called *More Than A Feeling*, this 2007 work by Scottish-born artist Jim Lambie is part of the museum's collection and sometimes on public display. That her place of employment has its own T stop isn't lost on Jen, nor is the MFA's value to her hometown. "I want young people and longtime city residents and those people out in the suburbs to realize what's inside these walls," Jen said.

EILEEN connors

To the many who have witnessed **Eileen M. Connors** in action, working with a nonprofit agency or a person in need, it is easy to see her compassion. But what some may not realize is that Eileen has long had experience on the front lines of human services. A former psychiatric social worker, she has served as a foster care and adoption worker, a college counselor, and a therapist. Eileen earned a bachelor of arts degree in education from Boston College, where she also received a master's degree in social work. She is a vice chairman on the general board of directors for the YMCA of Greater Boston, where she has served since 1997. She is a member of the R.O.S.E. Fund, on the advisory board of Rosie's Place, and is cochair of the advisory board of the Boston College Graduate School of Social Work. Eileen has been involved with the Leukemia Foundation, the Cystic Fibrosis Foundation, and the Task Force on Women and Boston College. She and her husband, Hill Holliday founder Jack Connors, their four children, and 10 grandchildren make up one of the city's most philanthropic families.

AYANNA pressley

When **Ayanna Pressley** was elected as a city councilor at-large on November 3, 2009, she became the first woman of color to serve on the governing board in its 100-year history. Ayanna, the only woman in the field of 15 candidates, immediately set out to support those she saw as underserved by forming and chairing the Committee on Women & Healthy Communities. Ayanna built her political career on 16 years of working for elected officials. She was a senior aide to former Congressman Joseph P. Kennedy II and U.S. Senator John Kerry. Just prior to campaigning for her city council post, Ayanna was Senator Kerry's political director, responsible for managing relationships with elected officials and community leaders. Involved in the community, Ayanna has served in the leadership of the Massachusetts Women's Political Caucus and is on the board of the University of Massachusetts Boston Center for Women in Politics and Public Policy, Emerge Massachusetts, and Action for Boston Community Development, Inc. And, despite her busy schedule, Ayanna is an active "Big Sister" with the Big Sister Association of Greater Boston. In the summer of 2011 Ayanna had begun her first reelection campaign.

MARIANNE leone

On-screen, **Marianne Leone** ranks with Joanne Woodward and Meryl Streep as one of those actresses who fully inhabits her roles. She was a regular on HBO's *The Sopranos*, playing Joanne Moltisanti, Christopher's (Michael Imperioli) mother, and has appeared in films by John Sayles, Nancy Savoca, and Martin Scorsese. As a screenwriter and essayist, Marianne lives the lives of the subjects she covers. Her essays and opinion pieces on a variety of topics have appeared in *The Boston Globe*. She is the wife of Academy Award–winning actor Chris Cooper and mother for 17 years to their son, Jesse Cooper, who she describes as "a warrior who battled severe cerebral palsy and quadriplegia." After Jesse's death in 2005, Marianne wrote a piece on grief that was published in *The Globe* with the headline "He Was Our Touchstone." Her memoir, *Knowing Jesse: A Mother's Story of Grief, Grace, and Everyday Bliss*, grew out of that essay. She and Chris have set up a foundation in Jesse's name to support inclusion and adapted sports for disabled people through the Federation for Children with Special Needs and AccesSportAmerica. The foundation also supports disabled orphans in Romania through the Romanian Children's Relief fund. Marianne lives on a tidal river in the South Shore of Massachusetts with her husband and two rescue dogs, Lucky and Frenchy.

LESLIE nordin

Leslie Nordin, mom to Sawyer (shown here, and the only male in this book) and his little sister, Riley, believes that her son, who was born blind, can take on anything life throws at him. She wants Sawyer to feel empowered, but she also felt a need to experience for herself the challenges he faces on a daily basis. So she ran the 2009 Boston Marathon—blindfolded. With the help of two friends and her husband, Dayton, Leslie ran the 26.2 miles from Hopkinton to Boston in a remarkable 4 hours, 17 minutes, and 48 seconds. And she didn't just run; she raised nearly $33,000 for the Perkins School for the Blind, where her son attends preschool. Taking on a marathon was not something new for Leslie. She began running while attending Duke Law School and, in addition to Boston, she has run the New York, Chicago, and Charlotte marathons. "I want to raise awareness about the abilities of people who are blind," she told the *Duke Law News*. "But on a very personal level, I hope to inspire my son when he gets older, as he grows, to set goals for himself that seem unattainable and reach them and do things that people might not think he can do."

Index

Kerry Brett, age 4, working with her dad, Bill. Photo by Ginnie Brett.

Acknowledgments

From Bill Brett

There are many people to acknowledge for their support of this project. I am most grateful to my wife, Ginnie, for her unwavering affirmation and love; as well as our children, Megan, Erin, Tim, and Kerry, who joined me as a partner in this book and whose emergence as one of Boston's leading photographers has amazed me and thrilled me as only a parent can appreciate. Thank you to my grandchildren, Morgan, Greyson, Hadley, and a fourth on the way; to my siblings, Jim, Mary, Peggy, and Harry, another photographer whose images have chronicled this city for more than three decades. Your love and support are invaluable to me. Two people who are no longer with us, my mother, Mary Ann, and my brother Jack were both inspiring to me in the way they lived their lives, and they continue to show me the way.

Special thanks to my closest friends, David Mugar and R.J. Valentine, whose long-standing loyalty and encouragement made this book possible. And to my mentors the late Don Bulman and Dan Sheehan—I can't thank you enough! My true appreciation to John Fish, Mayor Thomas M. Menino, Jack Connors, Joe Fallon, John Hailer, Joe Nolan, Bob Sheridan, Ken Quigley Jr., Jim Rooney, Charlie Baker, Don Rodman, Kevin Phelan, Joe Milano, Rick Kelleher, Bob Davis, Mike Barnicle, Anne Finucane, Heather Campion, Peter Smythe, Mike Casey, Lisa Hughes, Gerard and Ruth Adomunes (along with all of the great staff at Gerard's Restaurant), Bill Teuber, Kristan Fletcher, Justin Holmes, and Katie Archambault.

Annemarie Lewis Kerwin and Tom Mulvoy—thank you, thank you, thank you for your friendship, encouragement, and unbridled enthusiasm for this project.

Much gratitude to my fellow photographers and circle of professional friends: Ted Gartland, Jim Wilson, Jim Bulman, Stan Grossfeld, David Ryan, John Tulmacki, Bill Polo, John Blanding, Joanne Rathe, Suzanne Kreiter, John Ioven, Jim Davis, Wendy Maeda, Tom Landers, Frank O'Brien, George Rizer, Evan Richman, Justine Ide, and my niece Margaret Hastings.

Many thanks to the talented imaging technicians Susan Chalifoux, Jeanine Rodenhiser, and Cindy Meloski.

The Boston Harbor Hotel, The Liberty Hotel, and the Four Seasons Hotel.

I must also recognize Brian McDonough, Janice and John Schneiderman, Bob Collins, Ted O'Reilly, Bob Madden, Mark Shanahan, Meredith Goldstein, Bob Devine, Joe Davey, Tom Lacey, Corrine Ball, David Ting, Kelley Doyle, Jack Doherty, Steve Owens, Ed Walsh, Jan Goldstein, Dermot and Cindy Quinn, Ed Hayward, Ken Jaffe, Don Perrin, Ed Smith, John McDermott, Bill and Ed Forry, Peter Brown, Bill and Ed Balas, and the Sloane family. Your contributions, encouragement, and support for this project were invaluable to me.

Special thanks to Jennifer Hill and Mark Duffield, who introduced me to the founders and inspiring women at Three Bean Press—our publishers, whose guidance, creativity, and professionalism made for a terrific publishing experience.

From Kerry Brett

I am most grateful for my mother, Ginnie Brett, for her continuous love. She has made sacrifices for both my father and me, so that we could dedicate the time needed to follow our passion in photography. You epitomize the blueprint of the Inspirational Woman. I continue to benefit from your unwavering support and encouragement. You are the most inspirational woman to me.

.

My father, Bill Brett, you have always inspired me with your love of photography. I am so lucky to have you as my teacher. You have taught me so much and encouraged my creative aspirations throughout my life. You have always been my number one fan. I thank you for always being there for me.

To my daughter, Morgan, the true embodiment of love and joy. I am so blessed to be your mother. You are my best girl, and I love you with all my heart. You are my daily confirmation of the next generation of inspirational women.

To Danny Gallagher, the ultimate multi-hyphenate: singer-songwriter, comedian, actor, photography assistant, editor, partner in crime, but above all my love and support. You have a voice and heart that is as pure as gold.

To my amazing and talented sisters, Megan Khayali and Erin Brett, I love you both very much. My brother Tim "High Society" Brett, you have always been in my corner and there to make me laugh, and Tim's girlfriend, Liza Gorman. My brother-in-law John Khayali, we are so lucky to have you as a part of our family. Hadley and Greyson Gunter, my niece and nephew who brighten my day and put a smile on my face.

My uncles: Harry Brett (my other photography teacher), Jim Brett, my late uncle Jack "J.B." Brett (who provided inspiration to so many), Jack Sullivan, and Peter Dixon. My aunts: Margaret "Peg" McCobb, Mary McCarthy, Lucille Brett, Pattie Brett, Millie and Mary Sullivan, Clare Dixon, and Donna Sullivan. And to my many cousins and extended family, thank you for always being there for me.

Although this collection of portraits is a celebration of women, it couldn't have been completed without the incredible support of many men who have my unending gratitude: My mentor, Jeff Lubin; who taught me early on that "whether you think you can or can't...you are right." You have shown me by example that you can do anything you put your mind to.

R.J. "Dick" Valentine, who taught me to "never, never, never give up"; David Mugar, who truly demonstrates what being a friend means; and longtime friends Robert Karle, Ted Webster, Luke Magner, Tom Corry, Matt Delmonico, Brian Delmonico and David "Deej" Johnson.

My wonderful girlfriends: Jill "The Cosmic Queen" Jardine, you have been my light in my darkest hour; fashionista and fabulous friend Kelley Doyle; Sarah McLaughlin; Meg Gallagher; Anna Duarte; Erin McDonough; and my loyal "BFF," Christine Hitchens.

The friends who help make things happen: Kris Meyer, Kevin "Chappy" Chapman, Ken Casey, Tim Brennan, Dave McLaughlin, and Bobby "Bow Tie" Dougherty.

The incredibly talented artists and creators on Boston's burgeoning fashion scene Michael DePaulo and Denise Hajjar, thank you for always being on hand with your amazing couture, even at the 11th hour. Helen McKenna (Boston's best colorist) and Bridgit Leta, of ID Salon in Wellesley. Makeup artist Dianna Quagenti, model Arianna Brown of Maggie Inc., and Danielle Mignosa.

The überinspirational Marianne Leone Cooper, without you I would have never met my "soul sister" Maureen Hancock. Jennifer and Lenny Clarke ("Jen & Len"), I can't thank you enough for your kindness.

The Improper Bostonian magazine has been a second home, so many thanks to the Semonian family—Marion, Leon, Mark, and the late Leslie Semonian, and Wendy Semonian Eppich, an incredible leader and publisher.

Joe Heroun, who is a wonderful art director and friend, thank you for sharing your talents and providing inspiration that helped bring the cover to life. Nancy Gaines, my first editor, and the incorrigible *bon vivant* Jonathan Soroff.

This book wouldn't have been possible without the professionals I have been privileged to work with over the years. "Team KB"—the amazing Hallmark grads who have endured long hours and all-nighters, and for that I am grateful to Chris Rioux, Kyle Normandin, Lynn Gonsalves, Amy-Lynn Boucher, and master organizer Nicole Aiguier.

I have learned much over the years from photographers and friends—"superstar" Stan Grossfeld, Ted Gartland, Evan Richmond, Jim Bulman, Mike Casey, Janet Knott, Cheryl Richards, Walter Van Dusen, John Lenis, and cameraman Jeff Lazzarino.

Friends Ed Brunoli, Ted "Mr. Universe" Lopes, Nadja Pierce, Thomas Ashley Farrand, and Karen Paolino, thank you for all of your support. Taylor Groleau, who is always there for Morgan, Danny, and me.

The ultimate taskmasters and "gatekeepers" who open doors for me, Nancy Sterling and Meg Vaillancourt.

So many of the women I encountered on this journey have overcome incredible challenges, and yet they work so diligently to create change. Elisha Daniels and Kelley Tuthill continue to raise money for breast cancer, inspiring me on a daily basis.

The Gallaghers, my extended family in Raynham, are truly special and wonderful. Barbara Gallagher's words of wisdom make her an inspiration to her sons and daughters, and to me as well. I appreciate the continuous support from Kathy Gallagher Perry and her husband, Virgilio "Boo" Perry, Barb and Scott Murdoch, Tom Gallagher, Ellen Gallagher and Bruce Shetler, Frank and Debbie Gallagher, Andy and Annie Gallagher, and Chris and Julie Gallagher, as well as all of the kids.

I am very grateful for the team of inspirational publishers Seneca, Julie, and Sandy at Three Bean Press...talk about girl power! You are all amazing!

To everyone, I am forever grateful for your love and support.